WHY JESUS AIN'T GONNA DO NOTHIN
(BECAUSE HE ALREADY DID EVERYTHING AND PROCLAIMED "IT IS FINISHED".)

A message for you personally from the Holy Spirit...
typed by Pastor Allen Fleming

Never Judge A Book By It's Title . . . . .

Pastor Allen W. Fleming

ISBN 978-1-64416-644-4 (paperback)
ISBN 978-1-64416-646-8 (digital)

Christian Faith Publishing, Inc.
832 Park Avenue
Meadville, PA 16335
www.christianfaithpublishing.com

Printed in the United States of America

Dedication

This work is dedicated to the Author, The Holy Spirit. Jesus, in the person of The Holy Spirit, downloaded every word to me.

Jesus/Daddy God/Holy Spirit/The Word is my best friend forever, literally. We collaborated on this work as a personal message to you, the reader. It took a very long time to write this message but it was worth every bit of time, energy, and effort if even one of you believe Jesus.

Jesus is the most important person in my life. I cherish Him. He is my salvation, peace, joy, happiness, health, deliverer, protector, benefactor, and life guide.

I also dedicate this book to my best human friend forever, my love, Teresa. Jesus gave me the best wife in the world. The first time I saw Sweet T, I was cooked. For me, it was love at first sight. That was forty-six years ago. We have walked through nearly half a century together, and I love my wife more now than I did then. I recently asked Teresa if she would marry me for eternity. She said yes. Praise Jesus!

Acknowledgements

There are so many who made this book possible. It is difficult to thank them all. Here are the names of some wonderful Pastors, Teachers, Friends, Family, and Partners who have led me into ministry, inspired me, helped and encouraged me as I have evolved in knowledge of our Master and King:

Thank you to Jesus who is my BFF. We do everything together, and we crack each other up. He is so cool, and funny, and loving. Thank you, King, for my eternal life with you.

Pastor Dwight Keith, Dr. Mary Crum, Dr. W.P. "Buddy" Crum, Pastor Paul Crum, Evangelist/Teacher Jerry Thomas, Teacher John Michael Casteel, Teacher Ed Everett, Teacher Ron Reeser, Teacher Loyd Skidmore, T.D. Jakes, and Andrew Wommack.

My Uncle, hero, and buddy, Sir Captain J.D. Jim Fleming; My Grandmother, Annie Lois Stowe Fleming; My Irish Twin, Amelia Gay Nix; My Sister/Cousin Jo Hall Tiller; My elder sister, Kristie Walker, who took me to a place called the youth ranch when I was twelve; that is where my Bible study began.

My eternal love, "Sweet T." Reasey, Matthew, Lily, Ben, Meg, Ali Beth, and Jack; Henry Hine, The board of directors of Throne of Grace Ministries, My technical advisor and dear friend, David Parker.

My Partner, Mike Cottrell, My encourager and Pal, Brant Bateman, Mel McBride, Jim Lyons, Coach Jim Exley, Dwayne Samples, Bill Hobbs, Robert Velez, Dal Korn, Bill Gibson, Bill Wilson, Dr. Robert Smith, J.W. Manry, Dr. Michael Howard, Eric Swartz, Clay Meek and Joe Chao, Chris Eden, Scott Smith, Dr. Jeff Fox, Scott Garland, Strickland Holloway, My California friend and partner who wishes to remain anonymous—all of these folks have contributed to my Spiritual Growth.

MOST OF ALL, THE HOLY SPIRIT WHO WROTE THE BOOK!

Foreword

We urge you to read this love letter to you from your Sweet Daddy God to the last punctuation. In it, you will learn what Jesus is actually like.

This book has but two goals: that you learn to the maximum capacity of your heart how much God loves you just as you are, and That you learn and receive, by faith, all of His exceedingly great and precious promises, given you not by your behavior, but by His.

You will learn that your loving, caring, forgiving, merciful, kind Lord loves you personally beyond your capacity to understand.

You will learn that God does not do or allow evil.

You will learn that, regardless of what you have been taught, God does not punish or teach us by taking things away from us or by not hearing or granting our requests.

You will learn that God does not tempt or test us.

You will learn that God does not kill, steal or destroy.

You will learn that you have been given the same power as Jesus.

You will learn how upside down and backward our prayer life is.

You will learn that you are what God inherits, and that nothing that exists is more attractive to and cherished by our King.

You will be amazed to learn that God does not walk in the past or the future, and that the only time He knows is this present moment.

You will learn that God does not keep records of the wrongs of those who follow Jesus.

This is a prophecy given to Zephaniah about what life will be like for those who accept Jesus:

The Lord your God is in the midst of you a Mighty One, A Savior [Who Saves]! He will rest in silent satisfaction and in His Love He will be silent and make no mention of past sins or even recall them; He will exult over you with singing! (Zephaniah 3:17)

You will learn exactly what happens the moment the last breath is expended by our earth suits. We guarantee you that you will learn things about God that you never knew before. Good things!

Jesus taught us that if we continue in His Word, we are indeed His disciples, and we will know the truth, and the truth will MAKE us free. Many change this word to SET us free. The latter is incorrect. If you are set free, you may be recaptured. If you are made free you are free forever.

So Jesus said to those Jews who believed in Him, "If you continue in My Word you are truly My disciple and you will know the Truth and the Truth shall make you free." (John 8:31–32)

If the argument enters your mind that some of the gifts and powers you are about to learn of were only for the disciples, go back and soak in Jesus's oath that you just read.

Also note that the words Whosoever, Whomever, Whatever, Anything, Whatsoever, and Whenever appear in almost every one of Jesus's promises.

Please also pay attention to the fact that Jesus never qualified a healing, miracle or blessing based on the recipient's performance, other than their use of faith.

Jesus never said, "Yes but you must pray in His will." Nobody did! John wrote something similar. He wrote that if we pray in His will, we know that He hears us. Of course He does. Jesus always hears our prayers. He is not deaf. And if you truly accept Jesus as your King, you will not pray outside His will.

He has already given you the desires of your heart, meaning He will plant your desires in your heart that He has already given you.

We will discuss the fact that the vast majority of people pray amiss, asking Jesus for things that He has already given them or given them the power to do themselves. The Precise Unaltered Words of the Holy Spirit are the foundation for this work.

If at any point you have doubt about the veracity of the statements made here, verify each word for authenticity by checking them out in the Word. It is the desire of the Holy Spirit that His last will and testament be clearly understood. He wants His children to know precisely what He accomplished by His unimaginable love for (fill in your name) personally.

Jesus wants us to know and receive in our hearts every single thing that He bought for us. They are our inheritance, and it gives Him great pleasure to freely—without any qualifications—have given them to us.

Think of how much it pleases you to give a gift to a person who you can tell loves your gift and appreciates it. In fact, that is why you gave the gift. You wanted your friend to receive your gift in Love and Joy. You want that person to know that they mean so much to you that you thought about them, and having consider what they would like. You gave it in joy, expecting them to receive it in joy.

That is exactly how our sweet Daddy thinks.

Imagine the reverse. What if you gave your dear friend a special gift that cost you all that you had? You didn't even think about the price, you bought it as soon as you saw, and knew that it was the best gift your person could or would receive ever.

How would you feel if that person denied that you even gave them the gift? Or having acknowledged your gift, refused to even touch it?

What if you gave your wife a brand new Mercedes and she refused to touch the keys? How would you feel if your wife insisted on paying for your free gift? How badly would you be hurt if your wife, to whom you gave the great love gift, told you to keep your Mercedes, and that she preferred her 1963 Chevrolet Corvair?

Guess what? Your Daddy God left you your inheritance in advance! His Will is the Bible, and your inheritance is reported in the Words and Promises of King Jesus!

Regardless of what you have thought, been taught, heard, seen or read, it is a fact that God wants His children—every living being is a child of God, because He created us all—filled with Joy and Peace, and Health and Prosperity, and Grace and Truth, and Happiness and Mercy, and Kindness and Gentleness, but most importantly LOVE.

HIS LOVE!

We learned in our earliest education regarding our Father that "God Is Love." Is it not true that somehow, along the way as we grew, we were educated with worldly thoughts and became busy adults? And we heard different voices and forgot that basic truth? Please do me the favor of guiding your Atheist, Agnostic, Nihilist, Universalist, Science as a Religion friends or those of other beliefs to this book. Why? Because God cherishes each of them so much that He did all that you will read here, for them as individuals.

Using your imagination is fun. Don't you remember, as a child, saying to your playmate, "Let's Pretend!" Well, for you who are not believers, Let's Just Pretend, just as we did then with no bounds.

Let's pretend, even if you can't make your mind go there that God is very real, and that the Holy Bible is indeed His Dictation to the men who wrote it.

Pretend that God loves you so much that He moved all of the stars, galaxies, and universes to this precise moment,

11

just so that this Love letter to you arrived in your hands at the perfect time.

You mean that much to Him whether you deny Him, rebel against Him, call His Words a fairytale or worship other gods.

Peter was Jesus's friend. He lived with Him, followed Him, and witnessed all of His mighty works with his own eyes; as did all of the disciples, not just the original twelve. Peter wrote in the first chapter of his second letter to us these poignant words:

For we did not follow cunningly devised fables (we didn't make all of this up), when we made known to you the power and coming of our Lord Jesus but were Eyewitnesses of His Glory. For He received from God the Father, honor and glory when such a voice came to Him from the excellent Glory: THIS IS MY BELOVED SON IN WHOM I AM WELL PLEASED! And we heard this voice which came from heaven when we were with Him on the holy mountain (The Mount of Transfiguration) ... So we have a more sure (true) word of prophecy (the Words of Jesus) that we would do well to heed, like a bright light shining in a dark room, until the day dawns and the day star (Jesus) rises in our hearts"

We will teach about the mount of Transfiguration down the road a bit.

Please understand this! While you may be mad at God for whatever reason, if you despise God and religious people, if you hate people trying to convert you and when they do, it makes you even more hurt and angry; regardless of how you feel about God, He is not mad at you! He will never reject you, for any reason! Whether you deny Him or not,

God is not keeping a score card on you. He is not judging you or condemning you, and neither should any human, especially You!

God will always love you for eternity! You can spit in God's face, you can hurt Him, You can accuse Him falsely, You can hate Him, You can deny His existence, You can do hellish things and He will still love you for all of time!

Why? Because He created You! He knitted you together at the point of conception. Before that, He knew and loved you. He has numbered and is part of every one of your 300 trillion cells, infinite sub cells, and DNA strips of which you are constructed.

That does not mean that you can do those things and get away with them. The behaviors described above are evidence that you have not accepted Jesus and made Him your King. In fact, doing those things is proof of your rejection of God and Jesus. Once you make that decision, God with all of His power can do nothing to save you from the eternal consequences of your choice.

God has made provision for you out of His undying love for you. It is never too late to change. There is hope for you if you have done any of these things! If you turn now to Jesus and accept His forgiveness, you will be saved. What you cannot do is receive forgiveness twice. You cannot claim salvation and then continue in a life of sin.

No matter what you think, say or do, God is part of you.

Just as blood and marrow are part of you, so is God, The Holy Spirit, and Jesus. Even if God wanted to, He could not and would not remove Himself from your being. If somehow God could extract Himself from you, you would instantly disintegrate. Why? Because Jesus is the pulsating, illuminating energy that holds all things together! He is the God particle that scientists just spent billions on an accelerator to find.

No matter how you see yourself, whether you have low or no self-esteem or you are a completely arrogant narcissist or are somewhere in between, Jesus lives within you. And He will never leave you or forsake you.

The Author and I want to show you what is available to you if you choose to accept it. Okay? It will not cost you anything to finish reading. If you must, just hold your nose and pretend that every Word you are reading is true. You don't even have to tell anybody you read this message of "Great Joy."

You might be put off because what we teach is so contrary to what you have heard in a lifetime of perfect attendance at your church. You may own your pew and have had perfect attendance at your church, and have ribbons and gold stars to prove it. If you are willing to learn, you will.

It is possible that you may find some of Jesus's Word offensive because you have never heard them. If you do get offended, please accept our heartfelt apologies. Hold your nose and read on. Please don't throw the baby out with the bath water.

If you truly thirst after righteousness and right standing with God, we will show you how to achieve it. If you passionately love Jesus; if you have a deep, deep, deep personal love for Jesus, and a love for Him that is indescribable, and want everything that Jesus has; if you want to know and love Jesus more deeply; if you seek His truth without fear, this writing was done for YOU!

We urge you to please hear the Holy Spirit out. By the time you finish, you may think entirely differently than you do right now. Please allow the Holy Spirit to plead His case to you. Read every word of His love letter to you, and THEN decide what you choose to believe.

This very personal message to you from God may shake the foundations of your core theology. Know that there is no conjecture contained herein. What you are about to read is based entirely on specific teachings of Jesus, His prophets speaking on His behalf, The Holy Spirit, and the authors of the Bible, unedited.

We suggest that you get a good Amplified Version Bible. We use the amplified because in our educated experience, we believe it to be the most pure translation from the original texts written in Latin, Greek, and Hebrew.

Here are the marching orders given us by God in the person of the Holy Spirit:

Herald and preach the Word! Keep your sense of urgency, stand by, be at hand and ready, whether the opportunity seems to be favorable or unfavorable.

Whether it is convenient or inconvenient, whether it is welcome or unwelcome, you as preacher of the Word are to show people in what way their lives are wrong. And convince them, rebuking and correcting, warning and urging and encouraging them, being unflagging and inexhaustible in patience and teaching.

For the time is coming when people will not tolerate or endure sound and wholesome instruction, but, having itching ears for something pleasing and gratifying, they will gather to themselves one teacher after another to a considerable number, chosen to satisfy their own liking and to foster the errors they hold, and will turn aside from hearing the TRUTH and wander off into myths and man-made fictions. (2 Timothy 4:2–4)

You will notice that we never refer to Jesus as the Messiah or The Christ or Jesus Christ. That is because He is none of those things. Jesus was the Messiah, then He came to earth in the form of a human being and completed His divine assignment during His short visit to this planet.

He is no longer the Messiah, which means the one to come. He did come. That is why there is no such thing as a messianic Jew. One is either a Jew or a Christian.

If you believe in Jesus and make Him your King, you are a follower of the Way. If you reject Jesus, you are a messianic Jew because you are erroneously waiting for the coming of the Messiah. The Messiah will never come. He Came.

Jesus will return for His people, but not as the Messiah. He will come as the KING OF KINGS AND LORD OF LORDS!

When the Messiah was born of a woman, He became the Christ, meaning the anointed of God. So when Jesus walked the earth, He was the Christ.

When Jesus's body breathed for the last time, Jesus exclaimed, "IT IS FINISHED." Then He spent three days and nights finishing satan. Now His work is totally, thoroughly complete.

Jesus, after walking the earth for forty days and nights—after He rose from the dead, doing miracles in the presence of more than 400 eyewitnesses—left the earth to ascend to His Throne.

Now Jesus is no longer the Messiah or the Christ. Jesus has become the name above all names. He is the Alpha and the Omega, the Beginning and the End. He is the one who was and is, and is to be.

He is the triune God. Jesus is the name at which every knee will bow, including and especially His mockers, and declare that Jesus is Lord to the Glory of God.

Enjoy the Amazing Love and Grace you are about to gain!

Introduction

When I was a kid, I used to rush home to watch the Mickey Mouse club on our old black and white TV. It was nirvana for us kids. There were cartoons, Anette, Cubby, Darlene, and on Friday, cowboy/girl day. The show opened with a little tune that went:

"HEY THERE, HI THERE, HO THERE, YOU'RE AS WELCOME AS CAN BE!"

That is the welcome that the author The Holy Spirit and I would like to sing to you! You don't have to be a Christian or anything else. You are all so very welcome to enjoy this amazing writing about the power, glory, majesty, forgiveness, kindness, gentleness, and LOVE of our King!

In order to gain the maximum utopian joy that all of us seek, you must do two things: fully engage your imagination, and tear down any walls of doubt and unbelief, even if just temporarily.

Would you like to be blessed and happy, worry-free, rested, peaceful, full of joy and love, and wealthy beyond measure?

Imagine yourself being not guilty of anything you have ever done or will ever do. See yourself protected by Angels from any attacker of any kind. Imagine yourself free from all your cares. See yourself as being as healthy as you were as a youth, and staying that way all of your life until that time far in the distance when you travel on.

The Holy Spirit composed this book for the purpose of revealing to the beloved children of our Lord God Who He really is. His purpose is to teach all people, regardless of sex, nation of origin, skin color, language, religion, political view point, sexual orientation, denomination or any other distinction the truth about how passionately and eternally in love He is with them; and what He Has Done for them.

You are going to love this!

What if God/Jesus/The Holy Spirit was exactly as you had always hoped and wished that He would be? How wonderful would that be?

Suppose you were to come to know and love God in a very personal way, and you learned that He loves you infinitely more? What if it turned out that God is a Sugar Daddy? Have you ever wished for a Benevolent Benefactor?

Suppose the Holy Spirit whispered in a lovely tone in your ear, *"My precious dear child, neither has the human eye seen nor ear heard nor has it entered into the mind of humans the things that God has prepared for those of us who love Him; but He has revealed them to and in our spirit."*

How would you like to receive great and precious promises from your King, just by believing and expecting?

Would you love living and walking hand in hand through this life, and the life to come, with our sweet Daddy God?

How would you like to have a mentor and friend that would stand by you at all times and never leave you for any reason?

Do you wish to have a confidant to whom you can reveal, without judgment or condemnation, your innermost fears, worries, anxieties, and thoughts?

What if you actually had a God who never based His blessings on your performance? What if the only requirement to receive His blessings was to Believe in Him and Believe Him?

What if the Holy Spirit, through the power of love, convinced you that all the bad things that you have been taught about God were false, and that God is only a loving, giving, caring, forgiving, peaceful kind God who never judges or condemns anyone?

As you read, you will be astonished when you learn who Jesus really is, even and especially if you have been saved for a very long time.

If you hang in there to the end, as the promises of Alcoholics Anonymous state, "You Will Be Amazed Before You Are Half Way Through!"

If you read this love story all the way to the end, you will learn that neither You nor God are whom you currently believe you are or He is. The joy you feel will be eternal, and the truth will make you free forever.

BEFORE YOU CONTINUE, PLEASE PAY ATTENTION TO THIS NOTICE:

JESUS TOLD THE TRUTH or He was the biggest con man/ liar/fraud/lunatic who ever walked on the planet, and would have been satan incarnate.

As you read His teachings, and those of the other writers of the Bible who were led by the Holy Spirit, judge them by the preponderance of the evidence. Put all of them together and ask yourself who, but God, could have made up such a story? Ask yourself if you have ever seen more irrefutable inarguable truth and logic.

Let's hear the beautiful refrains of the voice of our King! They are found in His wondrous Word!

1

Let's Shoot Some HOLY COWS!

Before we can really teach you who God the Father, Jesus, and The Holy Spirit are, we have to blast a lot of made up Holy Cows.

These are paradigms that are absolutely false, most of which do not appear in any form in the Bible. I call them NON-BIBLICAL-CLICHES (NBCs). Many are phrases added to or qualifying the TRUE WORDS OF GOD.

Largely, these repulsive Holy Cows impugn the nature and character of our Precious Father. I am sure that you have heard some of them. No doubt you have believed some of them.

First, I have to write about a story that is told about two very famous baseball players. Don't worry animal lovers, my King and I love them as well. It is a legend that never happened.

The first player looked through blurry alcohol-soaked eyes at the other and invited him to go deer hunting at a friend's remote ranch in the wilds of Texas. As the story goes, it's 2:00 a.m. The boys are said to be quite inebriated. They drive for an hour to the ranch.

The first player called his friend and asked him if he could hunt his land. The rancher welcomed him, but requested that the player shoot his old crippled mule, because he didn't have the heart to do it.

The first player decided to prank his buddy. When they arrived, player one went to the door of the home and pretended to be having a conversation with the rancher.

He returned to the truck with a very angry look on his face. Player two asked him what the problem was. Player one reported that the rancher, a long-time fan who had requested many favors and gifts from player one, refused to let them hunt his land.

Player one tells player two that he is going to get the rancher back by shooting his mule. He pulls out a rifle from the truck and shoots the mule. Player one hears rapid gunfire behind him. He turns to find player two unloading his rifle and shouts, "What in the world are you doing?"

Player two states that he is getting the SOB back as well by shooting all of his cows!

Let's knock down some holy cows that are widely believed, but couldn't be farther from the truth.

Holy Cow number one ... Boom! Thud!

"GOD IS IN CONTROL!"

This is the Mac Daddy of all Non-Biblical Cliché's. How this crazy phrase ever got into the lexicon of Christendom is beyond me.

Let's just think about this in simple terms. If God were in Control, earth would be heaven! There would be no evil. There would be no illness. Every living thing would constantly praise the Lord.

If God were in control, there would be no sin!

If God were in control, every living thing would worship and believe Jesus. There would be no negatives. Nothing bad would ever happen. The planet would be ruled by God, and all would perfectly obey Him.

There would be no countries. There would be no wars. The government would be based entirely on love. Love would prevail at all times and in all places. Everyone would love each other as they do themselves and God.

Saying God is in control is the ultimate insult to Him. It assumes that he is accepting of murder, mayhem, and all types of evil doing.

Saying God is in control accuses Him of murder by negligence. It implies that God is complicit in the sins of mankind.

It implies that God needs to heal people. It implies that God did none of the things that He did. It implies that God is a liar, thief, and cruel beyond imagination.

This bizarre thinking implies that God was in control of the Nazi's and their collaborators when they killed six million Jews: men, women, and children.[1]

No statement in the history of humanity has been more inaccurate. It hurts my feelings each time I hear it. I can only imagine how God hurts when He hears these vulgar words.

God gave man freewill. Man's freewill is in control of this world.

God only has control of what we give him control of! God did not want a planet of automatons.

God already had all the angels he will ever need. He wants us to come to him out of our freewill.

"THE LORD GIVETH AND THE LORD TAKETH AWAY"

Everybody has heard, and unfortunately spoken, these words. They couldn't be more untrue. They were spoken by a destitute man who, through fear and unbelief, lost everything.

Job was the richest man of his day. Yet he lived in constant fear that God would take everything that He gave him away. His faith in losing his possessions opened the gate to the wart (satan) to take all he had.

This ridiculous iteration is a grave attack on the character of our Father who is LOVE. Ask yourself why in the world God would give something and then take it back?

[1.] Holocaust Encyclopedia

This errant phrase is almost always spoken at funerals, along with the twenty-third song which has nothing to do with death.

GOD DOES NOT KILL PEOPLE OR "TAKE" THEM!

Jesus went about doing good, and healing all who were sick and oppressed of the evil stench! Why would He then Kill people? Why in the world would God take something that He bought for us with His flesh and blood?

As soon as the revelation came to Job that it was actually his own fear that caused him to lose everything, he rebuked the statement!

He actually said, "The things that I fear the most have come upon me!" In so stating, he disavowed his previous statement.

Here are Job's exact words before he understood the truth:

Then Job arose and tore his robe and shaved his head and fell on the ground and worshipped. And he said, "Naked I came from my mother's womb, and naked I shall return. The Lord Gave, And The Lord Has Taken Away! Blessed be the name of the Lord." (Job 1:25)

Think on what Job just said. "God took everything I have, murdered my children. and put curses and plagues and disasters on me. Blessed be the name of the Lord" (paraphrased).

My guess is that he was being extremely sarcastic. The other option was that he was an idiot. Why would you bless a God who took everything you had and brought calamities and disasters on you? Thankfully it didn't take Job long to figure out how wrong he was in blaming God. By his inference that God did evil, He was actually judging God and condemning Him.

That did not sit well with God. It happens every day.

We will teach on the thirty-eighth chapter of Job later. Suffice it to say, God was not happy with Job whose ego was the size of Mars.

Here are the exact words of Job after his epiphany:

"For my sighing comes instead of my bread, and my groans are poured out like water. For the things I fear come upon me and what I dread befalls me. I am not at ease, nor am I quiet; I have no rest, but trouble comes." (Job 3:24-26)

Jobs words, "THE THINGS I FEAR COME UPON ME" are still the root of our losses to this very day.

Here is how that works: When we fear things, and allow the fear of those things to take root in our heart, we speak that fear out loud.

Because we have no doubt that the thing that we prophesy over ourselves will come over us, and we expect the bad thing to happen, we will have what we say!

Jesus put it like this:

"From the overflow of the heart, the mouth speaks and you will have what you say as long as you believe the thing you say will come to pass." (Luke 6:45; Mark 11:22)

You expect that thing to happen, so it will. Those things, positive and negative that we expect and proclaim, will come to be, because we put the forces needed for them to happen into action with our mouths.

Clearly, God does not cause evil or take things away from us. We bring these things upon ourselves with our unbelief and with our mouths.

The good Lord never takes away anything. He cannot. God cannot alter that thing that proceeds out of His mouth. To take anything that He has already given to us, which is everything we will ever need or want, would make Him a liar.

GOD DOES NOT CALL PEOPLE HOME!

Fear and faith cannot co-exist. They are opposite. Fear means that we do not believe God. Faith is the substance of things joyfully expected. Fear brings loss. Faith brings receipt of Jesus's great and precious promises.

It is completely understandable that you would not want any part of a God who gave things and took them away! Neither would I. Why would anyone love a God that ran over a two-year-old with a dump truck? Or burnt a house down to teach the owners that they don't need material things? Why would a loving God allow a woman to be beaten by a sick man or steal things or allow evil to happen?

Imagine how many people lost their salvation and/or never received the great and precious promises of Jesus because of this nonsense. How many people reject God without further investigation, because they have heard that He is so mean that He took their loved one or friend or their money or their job or their prosperity? Very sad, and woe be to those who perpetrated it.

I know two brilliant young adults who blame God for the loss of their Mother when she died in a car accident, because they have been taught lies about God. They believe that God took their mother. They want no part of a God who would kill a person. Neither would I.

SOMETIMES GOD SAYS NO, SOMETIMES GOD SAYS WAIT. GOD CLOSES SOME DOORS AND OPENS OTHERS, ETC.

Folks, God Has Already given us everything that we will ever need or want through the knowledge of Jesus (2 Peter 1:1–3).

"All of God's Promises are YES and AMEN!" (2 Corinthians 1:20; Hebrews 10:35–36)

These are the precise Words of Jesus about this:

"For this reason I am telling you, WHATEVER you ask in prayer, believe trust and be confident that it is granted to you, and you WILL GET IT!" (Mark 11:24)

What part of that PROMISE from Jesus sounds like, "NO, WAIT OR GOD CLOSES DOORS?" For God to say any of those NON-BIBLICAL CLICHES Would make Him a liar!

IT IS QUITE IMPOSSIBLE FOR GOD TO LIE!

GOD DOES NOT SAY NO! He swore an oath to Himself, because there was no higher authority that He could not tell a lie!

God never holds out on His children. The only time that exists in God's realm or ours is this present moment. The word *wait* is not possible in God's world. If God had never heard that word from us, He wouldn't know what it means.

GOD DOES NOT SPEAK NEGATIVES!

Here is one that pops my cork! Can you even imagine how angry it makes God? It is complete and utter stupidity. Yet, it is all over Facebook and social media. Here is an insane mad holy cow:

"GOD HAS A PURPOSE FOR YOUR PAIN AND SUFFERING!"

Whenever I see this foolishness on FB, I post back this question: "And just what would that be?" Jesus died the most horrible death anyone ever would to remove our suffering. Why would He then have a purpose for our suffering?

To believe such poppycock, you would have to be totally ignorant of the Character of God.

"YOU MUST PRAY IN HIS WILL"

This qualification is used by those who find Jesus's promises unacceptable, inaccurate, untrue, someone's interpretation, incredible, and in need of assistance and editing.

This whopper is used by those who do not know the Word or the character of God to explain why prayers go unanswered. The statement that we must pray in His will is not written anywhere in the Bible, and Jesus never said it!

The closest writing to this false statement is from John, the disciple of Jesus. John wrote a very simple, truthful, yet obvious comment in the order of (duh).

These are John's observations:

*"And this is the confidence we have toward Him, that if
we ask anything according to His will, He hears us. And
if we know He hears us in anything we ask, we know
that we have the requests that we have asked of Him."*
(1 John 5:14)

Please allow me to explain this statement. Remember that
Hebrew reads from right to left. When we believe Jesus, we
know that He hears our use of the free gift of faith. By faith,
we receive everything that He has already given us. Notice
that John emphasized that "we know that WE HAVE the
requests that we have asked Him."

Let's clear one thing up right here! If you have truly given
your heart and soul to our King, if you truly have bought in
to Him 100 percent, You cannot possibly ask outside His
will! Would you ask Jesus to stand guard outside the bank
while you rob it?

If you love Him, would you ask Jesus for your neighbor's
wife? If you love Him, would you ask Jesus to watch you
drink and drive?

IT WAS JESUS'S WILL TO GIVE US EVERYTHING! AND HE DID!

You will read this declaration from the Holy Spirit through
the Apostle Peter many times in this work. Why? Because
it is a cornerstone, and foundational to receiving what we
desire in our hearts.

Simon Peter, a servant and apostle (special messenger)
of Jesus Christ, to those who have received (obtained can
equal privilege of) *like precious faith.* (When we accept

Jesus by making Him the King of our lives, we receive as a free gift, the totality of His faith) *with ourselves in and through the righteousness of our God and Savior Jesus:*[2]

"May grace (God's willingness, ability and power that has done for us, what we cannot and will not do for ourselves) *and peace* (a state of being completely undisturbed, perfect well-being, all necessary good, all spiritual prosperity and freedom from fears and agitating passions and moral conflicts) *be multiplied to you in the full, personal, precise and correct knowledge of God and of our Lord Jesus.*

"For His divine power has (present tense) bestowed upon us, <u>ALL THINGS</u> *THAT ARE REQUISITE AND SUITED TO LIFE AND GODLINESS, through the full, personal knowledge of Him who called us by and to His own glory and excellence and virtue. By means of these He has* (present tense) *bestowed on us His precious and exceedingly great promises, so that through them you may escape by flight from the moral decay, rot and corruption that is in the world today because of covetousness and lust and greed, and become sharers, partakers of the divine nature."* (2 Peter 1:1–3)

WHY WOULD WE COVET OR LUST AFTER THINGS THAT WE ALREADY HAVE?

WHY WOULD WE ASK GOD FOR SOMETHING HE ALREADY GAVE US, WHICH IS EVERYTHING?

---

2. Note the receipt of the full measure of Jesus's faith is not about our right standing with God which we gain upon salvation. It is about Jesus's right standing. In other words, it is not about us growing, multiplying, expanding, adding to or building faith, all of which is impossible.

Jesus's promises aren't about what we ask! They are about what He has sworn an oath on His blood that He has given us!

One cannot, with any success, ask Jesus to do something He has already done! Without regard for what you ask in His will, HE HAS ALREADY GIVEN YOU ANYTHING YOU DESIRE! He put those desires in your heart, and He gave them to you by Grace.

He who did not withhold or spare even His own Son, but gave Him up for us all, has He not also with Him freely given us all other things? (Romans 8:32)

A promise to us by the Holy Spirit through King David:

Delight yourself also in the Lord, and He will give you the desires and secret petitions of your heart. Commit your way to the Lord; trust also in Him and He will bring it to pass!" (Psalm 37:4–5)

To ask God for something that he has given us is a profound statement of unbelief! The reason people have not received what Jesus freely gave us ALL things, everything by His love and GRACE is not because he has not already given them.

Why "believers" do not receive from God is because of their steadfast refusal to believe Him and His promises, and/or their ignorance of them. Ignorance of the promises of Jesus falls at the feet of those who should have known and taught them.

One of the key statements that will cause one not to receive the Great and Precious Promises of Jesus is this horrid cliché: "Believing For." There is no more obvious

statement of complete unbelief than to believe for
something you already have.

The primary generator of the lack of knowledge of the
promises of Jesus is the ignorance of clergy. It is a
generational and tradition issue. They teach what they
have been taught. Most Clergy are sold-out Jesus lovers.
They believe what they teach. Their teachings are in error
because of a lack of knowledge.

"YES, BUT! YOU MUST PRAY IN HIS TIME!"

More bovine excrement! God has no time! As you will read
later. There is no such thing as time in God's world! Time is
a man-made device. It is, at best, an assumption based on
a supposition.

The assumption is that a second is a second.

The only time that exists to God is this present moment,
which is His address.

If you just insist on praying in God's time, consider this:

*However, when they had rowed three or four miles, they
saw Jesus walking on the sea and approaching the boat.
And they were terrified.*

But Jesus said to them, *"It is Me; don't be afraid!"*

Then they were quite willing and glad for Him to come into
the boat, and now the boat *WENT IMMEDIATELY TO THE
LAND THEY HAD STEERED TOWARD! AND IMMEDIATELY
they reached the shore toward which they had been slowly
making their way.* (John 6:11)

How did Jesus do that? Molecular transformation! Jesus is the Ruler of all things seen and unseen. He commands atoms and molecules and cells.

That, my friends, is the reality of God's time. God moves at the speed of thought. So you see this "God's Time" nonsense is absolutely false.

Why is this nonbiblical cliché so widely used? Because people need a way to explain why (in their perception) aunt Mary has not (apparently) been healed.

Has anyone every run this hooey by you? "Well, sister, sometimes God says Not Yet?"

As is true for most Non-Biblical Clichés, that phrase is used to explain why those who Pray for things that God has already given them don't receive their petitions. The fact is that their very prayers sabotage the receipt of their hearts desires.

"GOD WILL NOT BLESS A SINNER"

This ridiculous cliché has another variant which means the same thing. Here it is: "Your sins will block your blessings!"

God will not bless a sinner? Really? Then explain how you earned your salvation. Were you without sin when you chose to make Jesus your Lord?

Please accept this teaching:

"God proved His love for us in that while we were yet sinners, Jesus died for us." (Romans 5:8)

Jesus died for all humanity, not some, not the Godly, not the Holy; but for every person no matter how lowdown or filthy or nasty or sinful they are!

Jesus can't undo what He did on the cross. He blessed everybody once and for all on the cross. He forgave all of our sins—past, present and future—once for all on the cross (Hebrews 10:10).

Jesus healed us all, once for all on the cross. He saved every human and everything on the cross with absolutely no reference to their behavior (Isaiah 53:4–5; 1 Peter 2:24; John 14:12–14; Matthew 8:17).

Jesus freely gave us all things everything we need for life— Godliness and prosperous abounding life—on the cross. Then He shouted, *"IT IS FINISHED!"* How then can he "unbless" us?

It is impossible to earn anything from Jesus, other than rewards in heaven! No human is capable of earning things from God by their behavior. Because we all sin and come short of the glory of the Lord. Nobody is without sin. Nobody!

That is why God placed us in a state of Grace through Faith, not blessings through works.

Think of a time when Jesus qualified a blessing or miracle or healing based on the level of a person's faith or on their behavior. Show me one instance where Jesus pulled out a scorecard, and after reviewing it, rejected a person!

NEVER is the correct answer!

"YOU MUST REPENT, CONFESS AND BE BAPTIZED TO BE SAVED!"

Pay attention to these teachings from Jesus and The Holy Spirit:

"For God so loved the world that He gave His only Son, that WHOSOEVER believes on Him will never perish but will have life everlasting." (John 3:16)

"Because if you acknowledge and confess with your lips that Jesus is Lord, and in your heart believe that God raised Him from the dead,"YOU SHALL BE SAVED."

"For with the heart a person believes in and relies on Jesus and so is justified and with the mouth he confesses and confirms his salvation."

The Scripture says,*"No man who believes in Him will be put to shame or be disappointed. There is no distinction between Jew and Gentile. The same Lord is Lord over all of us and He generously bestows His riches upon all who call upon Him in faith."*

"FOR EVERYONE WHO CALLS UPON THE NAME OF THE LORD SHALL BE SAVED."(Romans 10:10)

What you just read are the only requirements for salvation.

BAPTISM

Baptism means immersion; as to immerse ourselves in the Word of God. That is what God wants. He wants us to become completely subject to the rule of Jesus.

Visualize this. You jump off a diving board. When you do, you are completely immersed in water. Jesus wants us to dive into him exactly like that. He wants us to dive in with total abandon, not dip our toe into the pool.

Water baptism is merely an expression of acceptance of Jesus's forgiveness of our sins. It is not required for salvation!

Water baptism is a continuation of old Hebrew laws and ordinances. In the days of the old covenant, the Jews who were mostly agrarian wore sandals and walked everywhere they went.

The Middle East is very arid. Dirt and dust cling to the skin of those who are there. To fix this, they anoint themselves with oils and minerals, thus frankincense and myrrh, and the spikenard that Mary anointed Jesus with.

Anointing is refreshing and cleansing. That is why when Jesus was here, He was known among other names as the Christ; the Anointing, when we immerse ourselves in Him, we are cleansed and refreshed.

The water baptism was a cleansing ritual. It was a way of cleaning the dirt off of the body before entering the Synagogue.

Today we have showers and baths to accomplish the same function. In addition, we are not and never have been under the Hebrew laws and ordinances which require that we be cleansed.

Why? Because we have been made eternally clean by the blood of Jesus as we have been immersed or baptized into Jesus by our acceptance of Him and His Word. The more we immerse ourselves in the Word, the closer we are to our King.

There is absolutely nothing wrong with water baptism! It is actually very cool. Most people who do it are making a statement to all of their family, friends, and their community that they have accepted Jesus! Wonderful!

Only believe that there is no requirement for baptism in the Word of God. It has always been a voluntary act.

CONFESSION

Confession means to confess that Jesus is our salvation. It also means to verbalize how we feel about our King.

To Confess is not to report sin. It is to confess that Jesus is Lord! God does not need us to remind Him of our sins. He knows them. Our sins are past tense events that no longer exist. Our sins have all been flushed into the slipstream of yesterday, and burnt on the fires of heaven. They do not exist.

In the salvation scriptures you just read, did you find any requirements outside of believing? Did you read any qualifications? Do you see repentance, confession or baptism anywhere in them?

The false demands of baptism, confession of sins, and repentance from sins as a requirement for salvation are merely historical traditions.

REPENTANCE

The first time Jesus mentioned the word repentance, He defined it! Here, in His Words, is the meaning of the word repent:

The time is fulfilled, and the kingdom of God is at hand; repent and accept the Gospel (Good News). (Mark 1:15)

Jesus was speaking to all of us. In the Greek and the Hebrew, the word *repent* means to turn away. To repent is to change one's mind and turn away from wickedness. *Repentance* also means to turn from old behaviors and beliefs and accept the truth.

When Jesus said, "Repent and accept the Gospel" He meant just that, turn away from sin, consciousness, and the Law of sin and death, and attempt to gain anything from Him by virtue of performance; and accept the Gospel of Grace and Truth.

He meant for all of the Jews to let go of the 10 commandments/the law of Moses and the 603 man-made ordinances. He wanted them to understand and accept the fact that He was their replacement. He wanted them to believe that there is a new sheriff in town.

Yes, Jesus did also mean to turn away from sinful behavior as best we can. If we love Jesus, behavior modification is easier than it appears.

Jesus said that if we do not repent, we shall perish. Simple enough if we reject the Word of Jesus and His rule. There is no plausible escape from eternal separation from Him.

"GOD PUNISHES THOSE HE LOVES!"

This is a horrible holy cow!

Some very deceived people who do not know anything about the nature of Jesus believe that He whips and beats and punishes those whom He loves, harshly with disasters and calamities!"

Some folks, for whom have been presented an evil and inaccurate picture of God, see Him through their teachers eyes. They see God as a scorekeeping, mean, sulking, bitter, "waiting for us to screw up so He can punish us" God.

These believe that "God punishes His people" in brutal ways. They insist on it by twisting these scriptures:

"For the Lord corrects and disciplines everyone whom He loves, and He punishes even scourges, every son whom He accepts and welcomes to His heart and cherishes. You must submit to and endure correction for discipline; God is dealing with you as sons, For what son is there whom His Father does not thus train and correct and discipline." (Hebrews 12:6–7)

"He who spares his rod of discipline hates his son, but he who loves him disciplines diligently and punishes him early." (Proverbs 13:24)

People who use this scripture to justify harsh and cruel punishment of their children; or, to perpetuate a works or performance based relationship, are deadly wrong.

In both of these scriptures the reference to "His sons whom He accepts into His heart and cherishes," refers to sinful sons who have not accepted Jesus. Understand this: Every living male is His son, saved or not.

These scriptures refer only to those of his sons who have not accepted Him or His salvation. They are NOT referring to those who have appointed Him as their King.

"THEREFORE, There is now no condemnation for those who are in Jesus, who live and walk not after the dictates of the flesh, but after the dictates of the flesh." (Romans 8:1)

Child Abusers love these scriptures. They use them to justify "beating the hell" out of their children. This very moment, some perverted demon is beating a child and standing on that misinterpretation. This bastard even brags about brutalizing his children. He declares that God has commanded him to beat them with a rod!

Some misguided preachers teach these scriptures to their flock. In that flock are children who are being tortured by their parents. Some of the parents are drug addicted, alcoholics with no conscience. Don't believe it? Visit your nearby Children's Home and ask the administrator what he or she sees every day.

Does God correct us? Absolutely! Does He Scourge unbelievers? Yes, indeed!

The word *scourge* in English is a horrible mistranslation from the original Greek and Hebrew. It actually means to search us.

How does God correct those He loves? With His Word. Go back and read Paul's teaching to His protégé Timothy:

Every Scripture is profitable for: Instruction, for reproof and convincing of sin, for correction of error and discipline in obedience and for training in righteousness. (2 Timothy 3:16)

Ask yourself these questions as you read on. Does the Gospel of Jesus support a God who beats His loved ones with a rod? Does the Gospel of Jesus paint a picture of a vicious God who whips His children mercilessly, because

He loves them? Do you believe that God commands us to beat children frequently with rods? Does the God you are reading about seem like a serial child abuser?

If I believed that for one second, I would never have anything to do with Him.

If you spank your child, an act that I believe is less effective than other means, you are not necessarily a child abuser. Some however are.

"FAITH COMES BY HEARING AND HEARING AND HEARING AND HEARING AND HEARING!"

Some Television Evangelists, who are rooted in the teachings of Oral Roberts, believe and teach this non-biblical erroneous misinterpretation.

Along with this assertion comes the belief that you must improve your faith. It presumes that we must reach a certain level of faith to be capable of believing "for" a miracle.

If this Hearing cliché were true, how much time would you have to hear? How much hearing would it take before you got enough faith?

Faith is a free gift from Jesus! When we receive Him, we receive His faith! It is complete. It cannot be improved! It is produced by the righteousness of Jesus and it comes with salvation (2 Peter 1:1–3; Ephesians 2:8–9).

This teaching about hearing springs from a very bad misinterpretation of a verse in the tenth chapter of Romans. The entire tenth chapter of Romans is about one thing: SALVATION. It is not about faith!

Here is the truth as Paul wrote it. He explained that a Preacher must come and teach the Gospel, and that the Preacher cannot preach unless he is sent. Faith comes from hearing the Word from the preacher, receiving the Gospel, and the free gift of faith.

Let's read it together:

For everyone who calls on the name of the Lord will be saved. How then will they call on Him in Whom they have not believed? And how are they to believe in Him, of whom they have never heard? And how are they to preach unless they are sent? As it is written "How beautiful are the feet of those who preach the Good News? But they have not all obeyed the Gospel. For Isaiah says, Lord who has believed what he has heard from us? So faith comes from hearing and hearing through the Word of Jesus. (Romans 10:13–17)

Paul clearly stated that hearing comes through the Word. He did not write that faith comes by hearing and hearing and hearing. Read that sentence again: "So faith comes from hearing and hearing comes through the Word."

Made simple, People hear the gospel from a preacher, they believe and receive the Word, and when they do, they receive the free gift of faith; not based on their performance or repetitive hearing, but through believing and accepting Jesus.

How in the world can anyone construe this teaching on salvation to mean that in order to get faith, which in fact is a free gift received on salvation, we must hear and hear and hear and hear and hear?

The hearing theology is very ominous, because people hear it and believe that they have to hear continuously;

consequently, they spend their lives in total futility, trying to get more faith.

They believe that you cannot receive from God if you don't have enough faith, and they die trying to build up their faith to a level that qualifies them to receive healing and anything else from God.

Think about this: if it were possible to grow, multiply, expand, build, add to or conjure up more faith, how much growing, multiplying, and expanding of your faith would it take to receive from Jesus? How long would it take? Would a little hearing be enough? Or years of hearing? Or would it take decades of hearing? How would you know if you had heard enough?

Please! For Jesus's sake, if you hear any teaching that implies or overtly claims that you must earn something from Jesus, demand Biblical Evidence before you accept it.

Trying to earn things from God, anything, is not only impossible, but it innately requires that we earn everything from Him!

IT IS ENTIRELY IMPOSSIBLE TO EARN ANYTHING BUT HEAVENLY REWARDS, FROM GOD!

There are literally hundreds and hundreds of foolish Holy Cows. There are literally hundreds of Holy Cow herds. This is just a representative sample.

Can you think of some more, like "Jesus helps those who help themselves?" That one is a doozy.

The Angel of the Lord declared God's new deal to the shepherds guarding their flocks by night and to us until the end of the age:

"And the angel of the Lord (Gabriel) appeared to them, and the glory of the Lord shone around them, and they were filled with fear (Ya Think?)" *"And the angel said to them, Fear not (sorry mister angel, I already soiled my clothing), for* behold. I BRING YOU GOOD NEWS OF GREAT JOY THAT WILL BE FOR ALL PEOPLE!" (Luke 2:10)

If you hear ANYTHING but good news of great joy, it is not the Gospel of Jesus! It is most likely A HOLY COW!

Let's sum this chapter up by suggesting that when you hear something that doesn't sound like it came from your Daddy God who cherishes You above Himself, demand scripture IN TEXT as evidence.

The reason for demanding the text evidence is that some teachers give one verse answers, which miss the point that Jesus was trying to make.

Here is the last Holy Cow! Let's Blast it!

"GOD HATES GAY FOLK! GOD HATES THIS, GOD HATES THAT, GOD HATES DIVORCE!"

The Truth Is That God Is Incapable of Hate! He doesn't hate anybody, especially His Children that He created.

God loves all of His children. It breaks His heart when we commit abominations. It hurts Him when we behave in ways that are contrary to His system. All sin crushes His heart, because He paid the highest price possible to forgive us of those sins. When we sin, we contribute to the lashes on His back!

Why would we want to hurt our doting Father? Why would we do something that He has asked us, in love, not to do?

What hurts God more than anything is when a person rejects Jesus. In doing so, they judge and condemn themselves, and God is helpless to rescue them from eternal banishment. God Never Sends Anyone To Hell! His mercy is infinite. People send themselves to Hell. Not by behavior, but by the one thing God cannot change—Unbelief!

These are but a very few of the multitude of falsehoods that have been perpetrated on the children of God, largely by clergy. Remember, if what you are being taught is not Glorious News Of Good Tidings And Great Joy, it is false.

Now that you have a better understanding of our Loving Daddy God in all of His personages, it only gets better.

READ ON . . .

2

Jesus Gave Us His Eternal Love

"For God so greatly loved and dearly prized the world (You) He gave up His Son, (Himself) so that (You) whoever believes in, trusts in, clings to, relies on Him shall not perish but have eternal everlasting life. For God did not send His Son into the world to judge it, reject, to condemn, to pass sentence on the world, but that the world might find salvation and be made safe and sound through Him." (John 3:16–17)

Happy, Happy, Joy, Joy! When one accepts Jesus, He is made safe and sound through Him! We can now throw all of our cares upon Him! No more fear, worry, anxiety! We are safe and sound.

"As the Father has loved me, so I love you, dwell in my love!" (John 15:9)

Consider the Words from Jesus that you have just consumed. Jesus just told us that He loves us as much as God loves Him. God's love for Jesus is infinite. God loves you no matter who you are. He cherishes you! Never forget this scripture! When you accept Jesus, your sins are gone forever. God cannot even remember them. That is why asking God for forgiveness is so ridiculous. He would ask, "For what?"

Paul, our appointed teacher, wrote these so very beautiful and utterly true words about the love that our sweet Jesus has for us:

For I am persuaded beyond doubt that neither death nor life, nor angels, nor principalities, nor things impending and threatening nor things to come, nor powers, nor height nor depth, nor anything else in all creation, will be able to separate us from the LOVE OF GOD WHICH IS IN JESUS OUR LORD! (Romans 8:38–39)

IT'S ALL ABOUT LOVE!

It matters not at all to God/Jesus/The Holy Spirit, one bit who you are, what you have done, what you do, your religion, your unbelief, your race, creed or sexual orientation and practices, where you came from, whoever you worship. God loves you with an unending and eternal love no matter if you deny His deity or existence, if you are Joseph Stalin or Adolph Hitler.

If you are a bloody hitman for the mafia, if you are in a gang, if you run an abortion clinic, if you are serving a long prison sentence; whatever you think or if you revel in the things that break his heart, if you absolutely curse Him, and hate Him with all of your heart, God will always love you!

God cherishes you so much just the way you are that He gave everything. He had to ransom you from the eternal price for your sins.

He loves you so much that He died the most humiliating, degrading, painful death that anyone ever has or will, because you are the child that He would pay any price to have.

YES, HE REALLY LOVES YOU!

Did you find yourself being the only kid that didn't get picked to be on a playground team? Did you ever not make the cut? Did you ever sit on the bench? Do you remember how much that hurt?

Regardless of who you are, You made it on Jesus's team! Your uniform is crazy cool. You need only accept it and put it on.

Evil behavior is repulsive to God. It crushes His heart, but He has given man freewill. You may be heading to hell at the speed of thought, but He created you and loves you.

When you cast yourself into eternal damnation, He will be horribly saddened. He will still love you. You will always be God's child no matter how agonizing your end will be.

How much does God/Jesus/The Holy Spirit love you? Read Jesus's Words:

"No one has greater love than to lay down His life for His friends." (John 15:13)

YOU ARE JESUS'S BFF!

You are Jesus's friend. He is your friend. He is the friend closer than a brother who loves you at all times. He is the friend that King Solomon described in Proverbs (18:24), *"A man of many friends a friend of all the world will prove himself a bad friend, but there is a friend (Jesus) who sticks closer than a brother."*

Jesus and the Holy Spirit are the Paraclete, the counselor who stands beside us at all times. Jesus declared that He will never leave or forsake us. He told us to be at peace and know that He is with us, even until the end of the age.

Paul, in describing how much Jesus loves us, wrote this:

Now it is an extraordinary thing for one to give his life even for an upright man, though perhaps for a noble and lovable and generous benefactor someone might even dare to die. But God shows and clearly proves His love for us by the fact that while we were still sinners Jesus died for us! (Romans 5:7&8)

Jesus did not restrict His sacrifice to those who were "good." He didn't wait until we were righteous pew sitters in the First Church of High Holiness.

He died for us while we were deep in sin. He died for us while we were drunker than a boiled owl. He died for us while we were high on meth. He died for us in the middle of robbing the liquor store. He died for us while we still despised and rejected Him.

If you ever feel abandoned and unloved, if you ever feel that God is mad at you and could never love or accept you, if you feel that you have such an evil and criminal history that God couldn't possibly want to have anything to do with you, remember that He was brutally massacred for you.

If you are divorced and remarried, if you are a practicing LGBT or in prison for murder, and you have been told that God hates you, remember that Jesus died for you just the way you are. God loves you as much as He loves Mother Teresa, Billy Graham, and Bishop T.D. Jakes.

God is thoroughly incapable of hate. God cannot hate anything that He created. He cannot hate us. If he could, God would be hating Himself, which is not possible.

If you are a drunk and have lost everything and ruined your family, and you believe that what you have done is unforgivable, remember that Jesus died for you just the way you are right now.

GOD LOVES YOU! YOU, PERSONALLY!

So are you tracking with God, dear reader? Are you taking this into your heart? Are you understanding that God cherishes you above all other things? Do you get that Jesus died and took your punishment and all of your diseases into His earth suit, because He loves you so very much?

You are God's glorious inheritance! You are what He gets in exchange for all of your pain and suffering which He bore in His body. Yes, He felt every lash on His back. Jesus suffered the pain of the worst form of torture there is. He suffocated, was strangulated, and drowned in His own blood. He died of every disease known and unknown to man. FOR YOU!

Jesus was brutally beaten with the fists of Pharisees, Sadducees, Scribes, Temple Guards, and finally rock-hard Roman soldiers. He felt every single blow as would you. They placed a twisted vine of very large thorns on His head. Each breath made those pointed spikes pierce His head. He bled heavily.

He was whipped with a horrible device. The tips of the strands of the whip that was used to beat Jesus had shards of sharp rocks and pieces of small bones on them.

He felt the excruciating pain of every single strike, at least forty of them. They ripped the flesh off of Jesus's back!

Jesus was paraded through the streets of Jerusalem naked. The Pharisees, Sadducees, and the Romans wanted to demonstrate what happened to anyone who dared threaten their machine, so they brutally dispatched Jesus with extreme prejudice.

Jesus could have called a legion of Angels to easily destroy these cruel bastards. He chose to endure this. He suffered all of it as the price of having you with Him forever.

HE DID IT ALL FOR YOU!

The Jews did not kill Jesus! Jesus declared that no-one could take His life but that he gave it freely, for you! Jesus surrendered to these merciless thugs intentionally to buy you.

Jesus said this:

"For this reason the Father loves Me, because I lay down my own life—to take it back again. No one takes it from me. On the contrary, I lay it down voluntarily. I am authorized and have power to lay it down, to resign it, and I am authorized and have power to take it back again." (John 10:18)

Here is the exchange between the Roman Governor of Judea, Pontius Pilate, and Jesus about this:

So Pilate said to Him, "Will you not speak even to me? Do You not know that I have power to release You and I have power to crucify You?"

Jesus answered, *"You would not have any power or authority whatsoever against Me if it were not given you form above."* (John 19:10–11)

Important Note: For those who want to hold someone or some group accountable for the death of Jesus, they need look no farther than their mirror image. Jesus died for our sins. Every sin we commit or have committed had to be paid for.

The sins of each of us caused the death of Jesus. Every human being's sins cost Jesus the agonizing death His earth suit suffered.

THE MOST PAINFUL DEATH EVER

Though He was nearly dead and bleeding profusely from the whipping and beating, and was very weak and nearly blind from the sweat and blood in His eyes, He was made to carry the very heavy cross that would be used for the final, agonizing, unimaginable execution—more than a mile on His torn, tattered and bleeding back.

Along the way, He was spat upon, cursed, slandered, insulted, humiliated, scorned, ridiculed and mocked. He was shamed and chided all along the horribly painful path by the children He knitted together in their mother's wombs and that He had just been beaten senseless for.

Jesus collapsed from the pain and suffering along the way. The Roman guards beat Him and made him get up and continue. A man offered to carry the cross for Jesus, and the Roman escort knocked the man down.

He was hung on the cross after railroad-type spikes were hammered into His heals and wrists. Can you even imagine the pain?

God almighty, creator of all things, then took every disease known and unknown to Man into His earth body, which contained His Spirit, and suffered with them until His body could breathe no longer.

The deep gashes in His back, which quickly were infused with salt from His sweat, multiplying His pain, were the price He paid for our sins. This was the cost required to ransom us from an automatic eternal death sentence because of our sins. He suffered all of that to FORGIVE US ONCE AND FOR ALL!

Try to imagine what it would be like to have an epileptic seizure while suffering from scoliosis and STDs. Imagine having a massive stroke and heart attack at the same time. Imagine the pain of a cerebral hemorrhage added to suffering—Cerebral Palsy, Muscular Dystrophy, Sickle Cell Anemia, MS, Alzheimer's, Blood Poisoning, Cirrhosis of the liver, Brain Cancer, every cancer, huge malignant tumors and every other disease known and unknown to man—all at the same time.

Jesus did this to heal us all from every disease known and unknown to mortals. He did it so that we would never have to ask Him for healing. Jesus suffered this horrid death because He loves His creation so deeply that He cannot bear watching us in pain.

Death from crucifixion takes at least 18 hours of horrid suffering. Jesus was crucified at 9:00 a.m., and left His earth suit at 3:00 p.m.

Bearing all diseases, known and unknown, caused His body to cease quickly.

Jesus is not going to heal anybody. He can no longer heal you. He cannot redo something He already did. He is not going to forgive you again. He forgave you and paid for your sins once. You are forgiven by His love. To ask Jesus to forgive you is to crush His heart by saying that the price you just read was not high enough.

Asking Jesus to forgive you is telling Him in no uncertain words that you do not believe that He died on the cross for you. It says to Jesus that His brutal death needs improvement, and you are the one to improve on His sacrifice by your work.

As Jesus hung on the cross, He became all of our sins— past, present, and future. In His anguish, He cried out loud to God, *"MY God, MY God! Why Hast Thou Forsaken Me?"*

At that moment in time, for the six hours Jesus hung on the cross, He became pure sin. God could not look on Himself. The sins and unbelief that He bore were evidenced by His accusation that God had forsaken Him.

As His earth suit perished, Jesus proclaimed, **"IT IS FINISHED!"**

As you continue, you will learn in detail what that proclamation means. It is sufficient to know that Jesus never lied, and He meant what He said. This most expensive of all prices is paid in full. That is what Jesus meant when He said, *"Greater love has no man, than to lay down His life for His friends."*

IT IS ALL ABOUT JESUS'S LOVE!

Jesus gave His life for you so that you would have eternal life and live in a state of His willingness, ability, and power, which did those things for us that we cannot do for ourselves. All we need do is to receive His free gift through Faith.

FAITH

Faith is not complicated. Faith is the substance formed of living in this present moment with JOYFUL EXPECTATION, which is the evidence of us using His free gift of His faith (Hebrews 11:1).

Faith produces our vision, based on His Promises, of the wonderful, joyful, happy, "Zip-a-dee-doo-dah" life that He purchased for us!

Here is how our Spiritual Leader, Paul, taught this:

THEREFORE, SINCE we are justified, acquitted, declared in right standing, through faith, let us grasp the fact that we have the peace of reconciliation to hold and enjoy, peace with God through our Lord Jesus. Through Him also we have access, entrance by faith into this grace in which we firmly and safely stand, and let us rejoice and exult in our hope (Joyful Expectation) of experiencing and enjoying the GLORY OF GOD! (Romans 5:1-2)

How Cool Is That? No judging. No condemnation, no punishment; just receiving with Joy the things that we cannot see, though we know and joyfully anticipate, knowing that all things we need or want have already been given us.

GOD IS LOVE!

Beloved, let us love one another, for love is from God; and He who loves his fellowmen is begotten born of God and is coming progressively to know and understand God to perceive and recognize and get a better and clearer knowledge of Him.

He who does not love has not become acquainted with God, does not and never did know Him, FOR GOD IS LOVE. (1John 4:7&8)

Why would our God of Love allow a baby to die? Why would he allow a mother to miscarry her unborn child? Why would He allow cancer? Why would He punish us or tempt or test us?

Let no man say when he is tested (tempted), that He is tested (tempted) of God. God is not tested (tempted) by evil neither does He test any man! (James 1:1)

If you do not remember anything else from this book remember this: GOD DOES NOT DO OR ALLOW EVIL!

God pronounced His new contract with mankind when He was born as a human. He is no longer keeping score. Here is God's eternal commitment to all people:

Glory to God in the highest! And on earth, peace and goodwill to those with whom He is well pleased. (Luke 2:14)

God is well pleased with you! No matter who or what you are! Think about how much God loves you and how much He has given you because of that love. Are you beginning to fall in love with Him? If not, why not?

THE ESSENCE OF GOD IS LOVE!

God, Jesus, and The Holy Spirit lavish us with the love that we have been seeking all of our lives. No human could ever give you infinite and unyielding love. Jesus's love is totally unqualified and unending. Jesus's love does not judge nor condemn, ever.

God's love is never ending. His love has nothing to do with behavior or lack thereof. God's love is a love that cannot be earned nor taken away. It is a permanent, eternal love. Here is what the love of God for you is:

Love endures long and is patient and kind; love never is envious nor boils over with jealousy, is not boastful or vainglorious, does not display itself haughtily. It is not conceited arrogant and inflated with pride; it is not rude and does not act unbecomingly.

Love (God's love in us and the degree to which He loves us) does not insist on its own rights or its own way, for it is not self-seeking, it is not touchy or fretful or resentful; it takes no account of the evil done to it, and it pays no attention to a suffered wrong.

In that last verse, Paul said that love keeps no account of the evil done to it. It pays no attention to a suffered wrong. In other words, Jesus does not have a scorecard on us!

It does not rejoice at injustice and lack of righteousness, but rejoices when right and truth prevail. Love bears up under anything and everything that comes, is ever ready to believe the best of every person, its hopes are fadeless under all circumstances, and it endures everything without weakening. Love never fails. (1 Corinthians 13:4–8)

Our anointed teacher, Paul, wrote those words under the direction of the Holy Spirit. They are intended to be a guide for us in our relationships. It is, however, also an accurate description of how our Loving God feels about us.

Here is the character of God, again revealed to Paul by the Holy Spirit. We are to strive to be like our King Jesus:

But the fruit of the Spirit the work which His presence within accomplishes is LOVE, joy, gladness, peace, patience, kindness, goodness, benevolence, faithfulness, Gentleness. meekness, humility, self-control. Against these there is no law. (Galatians 5:22–23)

If you want to know the will of God, if you want to know who and How he is, re-read that scripture.

If you ever have self-worth issues, if you doubt your value, if you ever feel that you have no self-esteem, remember how much Jesus loves you.

A parting thought: ask yourself which of the alternative gods have ever claimed to love you this deeply and eternally. Which god gave His life for you?

"JESUS LOVES ME THIS I KNOW FOR THE BIBLE TELLS ME SO!"

JESUS SAVED US!

Saved us from what? Whatever we need to be saved from!

HERE IS THE DEAL:

God cannot accept any sin in His presence! We all sin and come short of the glory of God. None of us, even Mother Teresa, have the capability of paying for even the slightest sin by our performance. God knew this, so He became a human named Jesus.

God has four personifications: God the Father, God the Son, God the Holy Spirit, and God the Word. He is one hundred percent of each of His personifications. Think of it like this: God is all in one and one in all.

The Jews imposed an earth King and 603 ordinances upon themselves. They had demanded a King and Laws from God. God warned them through the prophets Moses and Samuel what these would cost them. They dug in their heels. The Jews placed themselves into servitude to the works of the flesh by which it is impossible to please God. Can you imagine rejecting God as your King? Seems crazy! Yet every country on earth has done that very thing, including the United States of America.

IF YOU WERE NOT BORN JEWISH, YOU ARE A GENTILE.

We gentiles were never under the laws of Moses (The Ten Commandments and/or the 603 attached ordinances) and we never will be, unless we ignorantly assign them to ourselves.

We, our ancestors, were lost and without hope. They were worshipping all nature of false gods or none at all. They were estranged from their creator.

Yet the Gentiles, those people who were not Jews, did have a path to salvation. They actually lived under grace.

If they sought God with all of their hearts, He would reveal himself to them. If they then accepted Him and turned away from their sins, they were saved by faith.

God could not bear seeing His creation implode. He could no longer live without (fill in your name). So he became a human by being born the natural way. Jesus came into this earth and into His earth suit by being born of a virgin. This was to guarantee the perfection of His bloodline from Abraham to King David, and King David to His birth mother Mary.

This was to fulfill the promise that He made to Abraham; that his SEED (Jesus), not seeds, would be mighty in the earth.

This is what Jesus referred to when He stated as reported by the Apostle John, "He who enters by the door is the true Shepherd." Meaning that He was born the natural way.

Jesus's birth mother was a virgin named Mary. Mary was a direct descendent of Abraham, Moses, and King David.

Joseph had nothing to do with the bloodline of Jesus. Think of Joseph as Jesus's adoptive father. Jesus's earth Father was God in the person of the Holy Spirit.

It was the Holy Spirit that impregnated Mary. And her genetics filled the earth suit of Jesus. God needed a human body to walk the earth. So he created One. That creation is Jesus. Jesus is God in the flesh.

God did this to usher in the new program of Grace through Faith and to abolish the old program of salvation and blessings through works.

"For as the law came through Moses, Grace and Truth came through Jesus!" (John 1:17)

You will read the definition of Grace several times in this message. Grace is God's willingness, ability, and power that has done for us what we will not or cannot do for ourselves. One of those is to pay for our sins.

What Jesus did, He did as an ultimate sacrifice. He paid for us with everything He had, which is everything. He did this for many reasons. Mainly because He wants us in heaven with him when our earth lives, which are but a wisp of smoke, end.

HEAVEN

Right before he went to be with Jesus, my earth father called me and asked if I would come see him. He said that there were things he needed to settle. At that visit, he asked me to describe heaven. Here is what I taught him:

Heaven is very real. It is the place where our Gentle, Caring, Giving, Kind, Merciful, Gracious, Glorious, Forgiving, Happy, Joyful, Sweet, Fun-Loving but, most of all, LOVING God resides. The Glory of God abounds in heaven. His Power and Majesty are in full display.

Heaven is so glorious and fantastic that it is written:

"Neither has eye seen, nor ear heard, neither has it entered into the hearts of man the magnificent things that God has prepared for us who love Him!" (1 Corinthians 2:5)

We know from the revelation that God shared with John that heaven is flowing with beauty, the streets are paved with gold, and there are twelve gates representing the twelve original followers of Jesus.

At the bottom or cornerstone of each gate are the names of a disciple, so that we can know that if those chuckle heads could make it, we can as well.

There are three beautiful gates covered with pearls in each of the cardinal directions. There are three on the north, three on the south, three on the west, and three on the east.

A beautiful diamond and glass-appearing river runs through it. There are magnificent homes there. Our relatives who were believers await us there.

Heaven is a place with no negatives. No sickness, fear, money, doubt, anxiety, pain or suffering, evil, sinfulness, hate, racism, competition, want, lack, meanness, bills, greed, gossip, anger, cruelty, insanity, politics or death.

In Heaven, everyone loves and cherishes each other. The past is gone forever as it is on earth. There is no time.

The peace in heaven is beyond description as are the joy, happiness, contentment, beauty, harmony, praise, and glorification of God in all of His persons. There is in heaven beautiful, soothing, peaceful, and harmonious music.

In heaven there are beautiful colors that we have never seen. There are wonderful sounds in heaven that we have never heard. Heaven is a bejeweled city.

There are dazzling stones of all types and beautiful breathtaking flora in Heaven. People in heaven move at the speed of thought.

THERE ARE DOGS IN HEAVEN! (Job 2:10) (Isaiah 11:6) (Isaiah 34:16)

The only requirement for entrance into eternal bliss is a decision to make Jesus the King of our lives.

Jesus taught us that we can build up treasures in heaven, they are rewards for what we do on earth.

Do not lay up for yourselves treasures on earth, where moth and rust destroy and where thieves break in and steal, but lay up your treasures in heaven, where neither moth nor rust destroys and where thieves do not break in and steal. For where your treasure is, there your heart will be also. (Matthew 6:21)

"Blessed be the God and Father of our Lord Jesus! According to His great mercy, He has caused us to be born again into a living hope through the resurrection of Jesus from the dead, to an inheritance that is imperishable, undefiled and unfading, kept for you in heaven!"
(1 Peter1:3–4)

"From now on, there is laid up for me the crown of righteousness, which the Lord, the righteous judge, will award to me on that day, and not only me, but also to all who have loved His appearing." (2 Timothy 5:4)

"And when the chief Shepherd appears, you will receive the unfading crown of glory." (1 Peter5:4)

[Peter is writing to those who will be around to witness the second coming and the ensuing rapture, but also to those who will transition to heaven between now and then.]

"Be faithful until death and I will give you the crown of life." (Revelation 2:10)

The truth is that there are infinite treasures that wait for those who serve the Lord.

Paul reported that to be absent the body is to be with Jesus. As soon as we vacate our earth suit, we stand in the presence of Jesus. At that time, we are judged for the good works that we did on earth and rewarded for those good deeds.

It is on arrival in heaven that we are presented with the treasures that we have stored up including trophies and crowns. We also receive our supernatural indestructible heavenly bodies.

Every child lost in pregnancy or born still, every child and every adult loved one who gave their hearts and lives to Jesus are in heaven. Every pet and every animal wait for those who are saved to arrive.

EVERY ABORTED CHILD IS IN HEAVEN!

Everyone in heaven is young. There are no old bodies. There are no hearing aids or glasses. There are no wheelchairs in heaven. No one frowns in heaven. If you haven't read the book *Heaven Is For Real* written by Randal Wallace, I urge you to read it. It is a wonderful picture as reported by a little boy who went there and returned.

There are, in heaven, crowns with jewels, astonishing homes, and at least two to three billion people who live in comfort and plenty of space. And that is where we will be forever if only we make Jesus our King.

In heaven, the Glory Of God shines throughout, and that Glory is the Light of Heaven.

Please understand what you are about to read is the truth. It is not written to scare you into accepting Jesus. He does not want anyone to come to Him in fear.

Jesus wants us to come to Him because of the Love He has demonstrated by making us free of our sins once and for all. This is why Jesus offers us a way of avoiding being sent away from Him for eternity!

NO ONE HAS TO GO TO HELL. GOING TO HELL IS A DECISION, A CHOICE. IT IS NEVER NECESSARY! GOD DOES NOT SEND ANYBODY TO HELL!

The reason we need Salvation is that Hell and eternal separation are very real. Let's clear up any false notions of what Hell is.

THE COST OF ADMISSION TO HELL IS NOT OUR BEHAVIOR!

Admission to hell is accomplished by denying that Jesus is God and/or rejecting His offer of salvation through Him.

Believing and/or teaching that there are many ways to get to heaven is another ticket to eternal separation from God. Here is a list of things that you will not find in Hell:

A way out, mercy, love, friends, sex, drugs, rock and roll, movies, entertainment, joy, peace, happiness, courage, beauty, LOVE, hope, grace, mercy, kindness, gentleness, comfort of any kind.

Here is a list of things that are found in Hell:

Atheists, agnostics, followers of false religions, anger, rage resentment, unceasing pain, bitterness, misery, perpetual nausea, torment, raging insanity, unimaginable heat, anguish, constant suffering, infinite suffocating fear, nothingness, eternal emptiness, unabated agony, horrid sounds, hopelessness, the absence of light, screaming, agony, wailing, moaning, immeasurable pain, horrid smells, filth, meanness that is indescribable, eternal misery, and constant illness without relief.

I have described hell to many modernists and biblical constructionists. They look at me like I have a giant dunce cap on my head and am riding a unicycle. They laugh and mock and decry these basic truths.

So very sadly, they will find themselves cast by their own choice into the hell described above. One thing is certain: they cannot honestly claim ignorance. They can't plead ignorance of the Gospel, wailing that they would have accepted Jesus if they had only known, will avail them nothing. There will be, at that time, nothing God can do to free them. But it is never too late to change while we have breath in our bodies.

Here is a fact: God never judges or condemns any of His creations. His love for everyone alive is far too great to enable Him to judge or condemn us. Men and Women judge and condemn themselves by rejecting Jesus.

"For God did not send His Son (Himself in the flesh) *into the world to judge it or condemn it, but that it might be saved through Him."* (John 3:17)

Muslims will stand before God and claim that they worshipped Jesus the Prophet. Like Mormons and Jehovah's witnesses and other false religions, they acknowledge the existence of Jesus but deny that He and the one true God are the same.

There will be many who cry to Jesus that they performed miracles in His name and did signs and wonders in His name. They will claim salvation. Jesus will turn His back on them, because they put their faith in their power and not in His Salvation (Matthew 7:21–23).

When the Bible says that God is the judge of the living and the dead, it means that His Being, His Nature, His Words clearly made known to all are the judgement of all.

Judgment and Condemnation are not Jesus's business. He exists so that His beloved children, all of us, can be saved from eternal separation from Him. He does not throw people into hell. They choose their eternal destination as an act of free will.

It literally breaks God's heart when any of His precious children reject Him and His offer of eternal life with Him. Especially because He suffered so intensely to keep them.

IN THE END WE WILL ALL LEARN THAT HELL IS A VERY REAL PLACE.

So God came to earth as a person, He obeyed all of the laws of the Jews, all of the Ten Commandments, and the attached 603 manmade ordinances which made Him the only person qualified to pay for their sins.

Nobody else ever has kept or ever will perfectly keep the Laws and Commandments. It is a complete impossibility.

Think about this: How are you doing on keeping the first commandment?

"I am the Lord your God, who brought you out of the land of Egypt, out of the house of slavery. You shall have no other God's before me!" (Exodus 20 verse 1 and 2)

This statement from God is as true today as it was when He led His people out of Egypt. He has delivered us from slavery to the bondage and futility of pleasing Him by works of the flesh.

From the Holy Spirit via the prophet Isaiah comes a teaching about the value of good deeds as a medium of exchange with God.

"For we have all become like one who is unclean, like a leper, and all our righteousness our best deeds of rightness and justice are like filthy rags; (I think if we use our imaginations we can surmise exactly which filthy rags Isaiah is referring to); *or a polluted garment; we all fade like a leaf and our iniquities, like the wind, take us away, far from God's favor, hurrying us toward destruction."* (Isaiah 64:6)

This graphic depiction makes it clear that our behavior, like filthy rags, cannot be exchanged for our sins! This will certainly be a shock to those who come before God proclaiming that they have earned blessings and/or salvation by their meritorious endeavors.

So many people are scurrying around trying to be good. They actually believe that such a thing is even possible. Some sanctimonious souls actually do believe that they are good.

They blow right past Jesus's teaching to the rich young ruler in which Jesus told the young dolt that no one is good except God! These poor, misguided, if well-meaning folk base this assertion on their attempts to behave in a way that they feel is pleasing to the Lord. Their conception is that God will hear their prayers, and if He is in a good mood on that day, possibly even bless them.

Bless their hearts, they think that it is possible to earn goodies by being good. My, how the holier than thou shall fall.

Which of course leads us to this train of thought: if we are to be good, we must at least keep the first commandment, right? How are we doing on having no other gods before Him? Most people claim that this is an easy commandment because they have no other Gods. Yet, how about work, the internet, television, telephones, movie stars, politicians, sex, addictions, alcohol, and exercise? These are just a few hurriedly thought substitutes for God.

If you still think you are keeping the first commandment, ask yourself how much time you give to God every day. Here is a measure of the position that God holds in your life: how much of your finances do you share with Him?

Try this experiment! Ask yourself if you would rather read the teachings of Jesus or watch a really good movie. Ask yourself if you would rather watch a football game or read the Bible. I suspect that you and Jesus both know the truth about that.

Often, people complain that my weekly teachings are too long. They take a maximum of thirty minutes to read or watch.

"IT IS FINISHED!"

When Jesus breathed His last on the cross and gave up His human body, He declared that, "IT IS FINISHED!"

There was a mighty earthquake, there was complete darkness, graves opened, and the dead walked the streets and were seen by many.

AND THE VEIL OF THE TEMPLE WHICH SEPARATED MAN FROM GOD WAS TORN IN HALF FROM THE TOP TO THE BOTTOM. (Matthew 27:51&52)

The veil that separated men from God was the veil that hung in the temple to keep people from entering into the Holy of Holies, the tent in which the ark of the covenant, the container of the original ten commandments, were kept.

That veil banished the Jews from the presence of God. In it were kept the laws that the children of Israel rejected God for. Only a cleansed and righteous Priest could enter, and only once a year. If He had any unatoned sin when he entered, he would die instantly.

In fact, just in case that happened, they wore a rope around their ankles with a bell on it. If they got zapped, the other priests would know what happened.

The tearing of the veil was to demonstrate that Jesus had fulfilled all of the commandments perfectly. He had rendered them complete. He nailed them to the cross.

There is now nothing separating men from the presence of God. His office door is always open. Now the only persons who are bound to the commandments are the Jews who reject Jesus and the poor fools who place themselves under them.

People get so angry when their paradigms are challenged. I had a discussion with a very stiff-necked "Full Gospel" man one time along these lines. I explained to Him why the gentiles never came under the law. The exclamation point of the discussion came as described above. My parting comment was that nobody keeps the first commandment.

The fellow went ballistic. His rage was that I proclaimed the impossibility of keeping the first commandment. His anger waxed strong and he belted out, "I keep the first commandment and all the commandments!"

Soon after, I got a letter from the Gent, proclaiming that I was in danger of going to hell for teaching people to not keep the ten commandments.

Non-believers who are not Jewish place themselves under a works-based system when they choose not to give themselves to Jesus. Works are their only chance.

There are not multiple ways to Heaven. You have to pick one. Abstention is not possible. It is one or the other. Either we choose Jesus or we choose works.

Jesus paid for the sins of all of the non-Jews (Gentiles) with His judging, condemnation, beating, whipping, crucifixion, death, burial, three days in the bowels of the earth, resurrection, and ascension to the Father. It was by His horrid death that we Gentiles were saved.

"And I when I am lifted up (crucified) *I will draw all men to Myself!"* (John 12:32)

GOD willfully allowed Himself to be tried, convicted, beaten beyond recognition, spat upon, dragged through the streets, battered and bloody, and to be brutally murdered— so that we will never be punished for our sins and that He can have (fill in your name)! He paid the full price for the sins of all mankind once and for all on the cross.

THAT IS THE DEFINITION OF LOVE!

Now, all we have to do to live with Him in Heaven in His glory for all of eternity is to choose to love and accept Him as our King!

Here are the scriptures dictated by the Holy Spirit that explain the program better that I can:

"For ALL have sinned and come short of the glory of God!" (Romans 3:23)

"As it is written: There is none righteous no not one!" (Romans 3:10)

"And the cost of sin is death! But, the gift of God is everlasting life in Jesus our Lord!" (Romans 6:23)

BUT…"God Demonstrated His Love For us, in that while we were still sinners, Jesus died for us!" (Romans 5:8) "For God so loved (You) that He (became a human) gave His only begotten Son (Himself in the flesh) so that whosoever believes in Him will never perish but will have everlasting life! (John 3:16)

"There is therefore now no condemnation for those who are in Jesus! The law of the Spirit of life has made us free from the law of sin and death." (Romans 8:1&2)

For the Jews, this means the 603 manmade ordinances and the Ten Commandments.

THE TEN COMMANDMENTS AND THE 603 ATTACHED ORDINANCES DO NOT AND NEVER HAVE APPLIED TO ANYONE BUT THE CHILDREN OF ISRAEL.

The great Pastor/teacher Jerry Thomas always says, "If you can show me where and when anybody—except the children of Israel—were placed under the law, I will eat this Bible right in front of you, leather maps and all!" It is a safe bet, because he knows that it never happened.

For more understanding on this, read the entire third chapter of the book of Galatians. Those of us who are not Jews were not, and never have been, under the law. Here is how Paul our appointed teacher explains it:

Remember therefore that at that time you were Gentiles, called uncircumcision by the Jews known as the circumcision which is merely a mark made in the flesh by human hands; remember that you were at that time separated from God, alienated from the commonwealth of Israel and strangers to the covenants of promise (the commandments and ordinances of the Jews,) having no hope and without God in the world. (Ephesians 2:11–12)

Some commandment storm troopers will respond to this message with this question. "Oh yeah, why did Jesus say that we are to obey His commands? Why did Jesus say that the first commandment was the greatest of all the commandments, huh, huh?"

Jesus was talking to the Jews who were under the law. They had asked Him which was the greatest commandment. He truthfully told them that the first commandment was the greatest of all commandments.

This is one of the most frequently misinterpreted teachings of Jesus. It is the mantra of the soldiers of the works movement!

If you love me, you will keep my commandments. And I will ask the Father, and He will give you another Helper, to be with you forever, even the Spirit of Truth (The Holy Spirit) whom the world (those who refuse to believe in or believe Jesus) cannot receive, because it neither sees Him nor knows Him. You know Him because He lives with you and will be in you. (John 14:15)

Those poor deluded folk who call themselves "believers," who in fact neither know or can see the Holy Spirit, twist this scripture to insist that we Christians are saved, but we must also obey the original Ten Commandments.

Jesus was clearly speaking to us of HIS COMMANDMENTS which are entirely different from the law of Moses and the old testament Jews.

Yes, those Jews who were before the completion of Jesus's works were responsible for keeping the Law that they had imposed on themselves. To them, Jesus talked about the Ten Commandments and the 603 ordinances.

When Jesus spoke of keeping His commandments, He meant His commandments!

JESUS'S COMMANDMENTS

Here is one of Jesus's commandments: *"Take no thought for tomorrow!"* In other words, live in the present.
Matthew 6:34

Yet Another:

"This is the work that God requires; that you believe on the One whom He hath sent." (John 6:29)

That commandment set the world on fire! The Jews had just tried to get Jesus to tell them that the way of salvation was their beloved laws handed down to them by Moses. They asked Jesus what God required of them.

Jesus actually stood in a high holy Synagogue and told the Priests, Scribes, Pharisees, and congregants that their Laws, which they cherished but never kept, were done. And that He was the replacement for them!

The crowd went nuts like progressives at a Trump rally or conservatives watching an Obama state of the Union address. His disciples ran for cover, never to return. All you could see of Jesus's followers were backsides and elbows.

"BLASPHEMER!" was the label that Jesus earned with that declaration.

The twelve almost ran away with the rest of the disciples, but they didn't know where they could hide from God. They were, however, petrified and asked Jesus if He was nuts! They implied that Jesus was going to get them all killed!

You have got to read about this. It is one of the funniest events in history! No doubt, Daddy God was rolling on the floor of Heaven laughing hysterically! The Law thumpers of that day were no different than many clergy of today when confronted with the truth of the promises of Jesus. If you want a deep belly laugh, read this news report in John 6:28–62.

Be careful not to judge the unbelief of others until you have read the unedited promises of Jesus in this book. You will know for sure if you are with Jesus or the runners if you stop reading or discard this message.

We all need a really long hard laugh. That is why Solomon in his great wisdom proclaimed that "a merry heart does good like a medicine."

This scene is funnier than Chris Farley in the van down by the river or when Joe Pesci put his head in the kerosene-filled toilet in *Home Alone 2*. Stop now and open your Bible and read. It takes a few minutes because it is a long message, but read it all the way to the question at verse 62. When you finish verse 62, immediately go to Acts 1:9–11.

I plead with you to do this right now! When you stop laughing, come back and finish this chapter. I dare anybody to tell me that God is not funnier than anyone you have ever seen or heard. The funniest part is what the angels asked the disciples while trying not to bust out in hysterics themselves.

Yet another commandment from Jesus:

"Seek ye first the Kingdom of God, and its righteousness (Jesus) then all these things shall be added unto you." (Matthew 6:33)

There is a distinct cause and effect to this promise of Jesus. When you seek first the kingdom of God, which is Jesus, you do so in faith. It is by faith that we receive all of the Great and Precious Promises of Jesus.

Another:

So then, Whatever you desire that others would do to and for you, even so do also to and for them, for this sums up the law and the prophets. (Matthew 7:12)

We have all heard this one:

DO NOT judge and criticize and condemn others, so that you may not be judged and criticized and condemned yourselves. For just as you judge and criticize and condemn others, you will be judged and criticized and condemned, and with the measure that you use to deal out to others, it will be dealt out again to you. (Matthew 7:1–2)

This instruction is true about everything you do! If you give love, you get love returned to you with the same measure you give. If you give money, you receive back with the measure you give. If you give little, you get little; if you give much, you get much. These are cornerstone truths created by God. They are unchangeable.

How are we doing on this command from Jesus?

"A new command I give you. As I have loved you, love one another. By this people will know that you are my disciples." (John 13:34–35)

Jesus gave us many very cool and wise commandments. Look them up and learn them. They are located in the first four books of the New Testament. God does not punish us for not keeping them. Our lives are made better and we are drawn closer to our Loving Jesus when we do.

Here is the kicker:

"And there is salvation in no one else, for there is no name under heaven given among men, by which we must be saved." (Acts 4:12)

The previous scripture would include buddha, animals, idols, mohammed or any false Gods. It means that Jesus is the only way! Some people, for reasons that I cannot understand, find the following Words of Jesus disturbing and offensive and untrue:

"I AM THE WAY, AND THE TRUTH, AND THE LIFE, NO MAN COMES TO THE FATHER, BUT BY ME! If you had known Me, you should have known My Father. From now on you know Him and have seen Him!" (John 14:7–8)

There are many people who call themselves liberal Christians. They have an extremely flawed, false theology. Their man made construct is a bastardization of the truth. It is that, "THERE ARE MANY WAYS TO GET TO HEAVEN."

Some of the most widely known celebrities have been spewing this bovine excrement for years. They will pay an everlasting price for this, because they have caused thousands, if not millions, to lose their salvation by rejecting the deity of Jesus—including their own. They are not Christians at all. They are universalists, and little do they know they are condemned to eternal separation from God!

Think about this! If Jesus is not God, He cannot have forgiven us our sins. Therefore, we must earn salvation by our actions, which is utter nonsense. I pity these poor revisionists. They created their ridiculous premise because they want to live any way they choose. Most of them actually are so deceived that they believe that they are intellectually and morally superior to God.

UNPARDONABLE SINS

There are only four unpardonable sins:

(1) REJECTING THE DIETY OF JESUS. Believing and declaring that Jesus was "a good man," a "prophet," the Son of God, but not a deity, etc.

(2) APOSTASY. Having accepted Jesus, rejecting Him seriously and or publicly, i.e. converting to Islam, Judaism, Buddhism, Hindi, Wicca or another philosophy or religion. This is known as the sin of Apostasy.

Paul writing in the book of Hebrews under the direction of the Holy Spirit:

For it is impossible, [to restore and bring again to repentance] those who have once been enlightened, who have tasted the heavenly gift, and have shared in the Holy Spirit, and have consciously tasted the goodness of the Word of God and the powers of the world to come, and then have fallen away; to restore their own again to repentance (changing of belief and behavior) since they are crucifying once again the Son of God to their harm and holding Him up to contempt. (Hebrews 6:4–8)

(3) GRIEVING THE HOLY SPIRIT. Such as mocking God, mocking believers, mocking the Bible and it's contents, preaching that Jesus is not the only way to salvation. Placing a crucifix in a bottle of urine would fall under the category of grieving the Holy Spirit.

(4) UNBELIEF. Refusing to accept or believe the Gospel of Jesus.

Works pounders always sarcastically ask me the same lame question, "So I can do anything I want and it will be okay?"

Here is the answer: No! If you have truly made Jesus the King of your life, if you are truly submitted completely to our sweet Lord, you are not going to behave outside of His will!

This is how the Holy Spirit writing through Paul answered this very question:

"What then are we to conclude? Shall we sin because we live not under Law but under God's favor and mercy? Certainly not!" (Romans 6:15)

No one can accurately claim Jesus and shoot another person or commit rape or theft. All of us will behave badly and sin; even so, our sins are forgiven us if we have made Jesus our King. "Christians" sin! None of us are without sin. Those, however, who live lives of continuous sin so that sin becomes a lifestyle will never convince me that they have accepted Jesus.

Works troopers believe that you can lose your salvation based on your behavior, and they couldn't possibly be more wrong! They call it "backsliding." It is the silliest of all beliefs.

Imagine God granting us salvation then taking it back! Ridiculous! How would that be accomplished? Would Jesus turn back time and jump down off the cross? Here is how our sins get wiped out—past, present, and future—once and forever.

SALVATION 101

"If you acknowledge and confess with your lips that Jesus is Lord (and mean it, if you give Jesus command and control over everything in your life) and in your heart believe that God raised Him from the dead ... YOU WILL BE SAVED!"

Those are the Only requirements of God for us to join Him forever. Contrary to the common paradigm, you don't have to fall on your knees and report to God every sin you have ever committed, repent, and ask God to forgive you. He already forgave us and He knows all of our sins. You don't have to remind Him of them.

When Jesus said, *"Repent and accept the Gospel,"* He was talking to old covenant Jews who were bound to the law. He was commanding them to let go of the law, turn from it, and accept the fact that the game has changed. Jesus wanted them to believe and accept Him, and understand that He is the replacement for the 603 manmade regulations and the commandments given them by Moses.

When the Jews rejected God ten times in the desert on the way to the land flowing with milk and honey, and sinned against God, they brought the impossible to keep laws on themselves.

Paul taught us that the Ten Commandments and the ordinances were the Law of sin and death. He taught us that they were added to or put on the Jews because of their transgressions. Specifically, rejecting God.

God knew their thoughts. He knew that they would reject Jesus, just as they had rejected Him. They had done it ten times immediately after He had done ten amazing miracles to gain their freedom from Egypt. As a matter of fact, they refused to be led by God and spoken to by Him. They actually rejected God for a king and laws, and that was their downfall.

Here is what went down.

Then all the elders of Israel gathered together and came to Samuel at Ramah and said to him, Behold you are old and your sons do not walk in your ways. Now appoint a King for us to judge us like all the nations. But the thing displeased Samuel when they said, "Give us a king to judge us." And Samuel prayed to the Lord. And the Lord said to Samuel, "Obey the voice of the people in all that they say to you, for they have not rejected you, but they have rejected Me from being king over them." (1 Samuel:4–7)

They actually told God that they would not listen to Him, only Moses. From that day on, they only heard God through prophets.

And the people said to Moses, "You speak to us and we will listen, but do not let God speak to us lest we die." (Exodus 20:19)

A LESSON ON CONFESSION

Let's discuss confession and repentance and what they mean! Confession is not reporting to Jesus every sin we commit. Does anyone actually believe that Jesus is unaware of the sins they have committed? Jesus meant that He wants to know what our confession is.

The confession that God requires is this: "Jesus is my King! I accept Him honestly and completely!" The only required confession is this one:

If you confess with your mouth that Jesus is Lord and believe in your heart that God raised Him from the dead you shall be saved. For with the heart a person believes and so is justified and declared righteous (in right standing with God) and with the mouth he confesses, declares openly and speaks out freely his faith, and confirms his salvation. (Romans 10:9–10)

That is the only confession you ever need make. John the disciple confused many people when he wrote:

"If we say we have no sin, we deceive ourselves, and the truth is not in us. (true, we all sin). If we confess our sins, He is faithful and just to forgive our sins and to cleanse us from all unrighteousness. (1 John 1:8–9)

THAT VERSE IS NOT ABOUT CONFESSING! IT IS ABOUT ADMITTING THAT WE HAVE SIN IN OUR LIVES AND NEED A SAVIOR. THE MOMENT WE DO, AND MAKE JESUS OUR KING, WE RECEIVE HIS ETERNAL FORGIVENESS AND ARE IMMEDIATELY CLEANSED ONCE AND FOR ALL OF ALL UNRIGHTEOUSNESS. IT IS ABOUT ACCEPTING JESUS AND ADMITTING OUR NEED FOR HIM ONCE.

Entire denominations have misunderstood this scripture and have perpetuated their misunderstanding continually since they started.

They have taught incorrectly all of that time that John meant that we must confess all of our sins.

Paul declared firmly that all of our sins—past, present, and future—have been forgiven by the sacrifice of Jesus once and for all. Here is what he wrote:

And in accordance with the will of God, we have been made holy, consecrated and sanctified through the offering made ONCE FOR ALL, of the body of Jesus! (Hebrews 10:10)

John did not mean as some denominations insist that we must play a continuous game of musical chairs, confessing every sin every time we sin, and hoping that we don't croak before we confess our last sin. Because in their belief, if that happens, you are doomed to hell.

AN EXAMPLE OF CONFESSION

There is another meaning of confession. God loves to hear our personal confessions about Him. They are not required. He wants them to be created by our love for Him.

Jesus asked the disciples, *"Who is it that you say I am?"* He wanted their personal confession of who He was. The greatest personal confession is the twenty-third Psalm. It is King David's confession of who the Triune God is and what He means to him. Here is David's love letter and unchanging, inalterable CONFESSION:

The Lord is my shepherd; I shall NOT want (lack anything ever)! He makes me lie down in green pastures. (You cannot be wealthier and more prosperous as a sheep, than to lie down in green pastures) He leads me beside still waters. (Sheep are skittish and fretful and nervous and anxious, as are we. Moving waters scare them. God leads us beside the peaceful quiet waters, if we will follow Him.) *He leads me in the paths of righteousness for His name's sake.* So that others will see our right standing and desire to live in right standing also, by accepting Jesus. It also means that the Lord has led us to Himself in the person of Jesus and when we accept Him we have the same right standing with God that He has. *Even though I walk through*

THE VALLEY OF SHADOW of evil, I will fear no evil, for You are with me, Your Rod (Jesus) and Your Staff (The Holy Spirit) they comfort me. We never walk through the valley of death. Merely the shadow of death. It is impossible for a Jesus follower to die! *You prepare a table for me in the presence of my enemies.* God lays out a feast for us in the presence of our enemy. While he is saber rattling, we are mocking him by munching on lobster right in front of him, to clearly demonstrate how unconcerned we are, because it's not our fight it's God's fight!

David proclaimed that God does not merely bless us and greet us as His most honored guest, He blesses us with lavishness and abundance until our cups run over. In those days, when the guest of honor arrived, his head was anointed with the most refreshing oils. It was a symbol of how highly the host regarded his guest. The cup to which he refers is known as a chin cup. It was used to capture any overflow from the head and beard anointing.

The word *Christ* means the anointed or the anointing. When we have Jesus, he becomes the refreshing, cleansing, rejuvenating newness of life that we seek.

Surely Goodness and Mercy shall follow me all the days of my life, and I shall dwell in the house of the Lord forever!

David knew that this statement is absolute fact, not because of his behavior. David was a murderer, a thief, an adulterer, a liar, and a voyeur. Yet God called him a man after his own heart. God, forgave and cherished David, because David was madly in love with God. David knew that He was saved by grace through faith just as we are.

The twenty-third Psalm is one of David's many confessions about God. Oddly, David's confession—overflowing with love, joy, happiness, and abundant life—is frequently read at all places, funerals and memorial services. It has nothing at all to do with death; rather, it is about love and life!

REPENTENCE

When Jesus asks us to repent, He means to reject any other beliefs. He wants us to accept His salvation, His promises, and His Love. Jesus wants everyone to be with Him for all of eternity, and the only way to do that is to turn away from other religions and accept Him.

If you are hearing a Gospel that is not good news, drop it like a hot rock! Repent! Run to the love of Jesus! If what you are being taught is that God allows evil or does evil, don't hesitate; run like an angry Grizzly bear is chasing you.

If you are hearing and believing any Gospel that is not GOOD NEWS OF GREAT JOY FOR ALL THE PEOPLE, repent and turn to the truth.

If you worship any other god or belief or are agnostic or atheist or nihilist, repent; turn to the Gospel of Jesus. You will find more peace, joy, love, acceptance, and happiness than you have ever dreamt possible.

Repentance from lives of willful sinfulness comes with giving our lives to Jesus. When we love and obey Jesus, we will change our bad behavior and act in a way that would please Him; not under penalty of punishment if we don't behave well, but out of LOVE.

REPENT. Reject any belief than that the Gospel of Jesus is untrue. If you want true happiness and peace in your life, be truly grateful for the Love of God who cherishes you above anything else He created.

Get into the habit of thanking Jesus every day for His incomprehensible love, which caused Him to give us everything we will ever have, want or need.

Study His Word, which is Him, no matter how many times you have read or how long you have studied the Bible. Start all over with a sense of love and gratitude. Start in the first chapter and first verse of the Book written by the Apostle John.

Jesus taught us that the more we study and learn who He is, the more we will know and receive. When you truly begin to learn who Jesus really is and what He actually taught, the more you will fall into a deep and passionate love with Him.

The following scripture is the great teacher Ron Reeser's favorite teaching, because it is so important. Through it, you receive blessing upon blessing to infinity:

And He said to them, "Be careful what you are hearing. The measure of thought and study you give to the truth you hear will be the measure of virtue and knowledge that comes back to you — and more besides will be given to you who hear." (Mark 4:24)

Ask the Holy Spirit to bring you to a complete understanding of the Word as you consume it. Make the Words of Jesus the energy source of your life. (Psalm 23) Make a decision to believe them beyond the shadow of a doubt! What have you got to lose?

There is a question called "Pascal's Wager." The question is, what do you have to lose by accepting that Jesus and God and the Holy Spirit are? And that they are rewarders of those who diligently seek them? (Hebrews 11:6).

Are you willing to gamble eternal hell and separation from God? Against abounding joy, prosperity, peace, and happiness now and in the life to come? Do you actually believe that you are intellectually and morally superior to God? Some do. How very sad. The most miserable scene that I have ever witnessed was the funeral of an atheist.

Are you of another faith? I have studied many religions— Judaism, Hinduism, Islam, Buddhism and other Asian religions—and many philosophies and psychologists. The result is a discovery that no other religion, belief system, god or philosophy GUARANTEES a person eternal salvation.

It is true that you can be saved by performance. You do not need the intercession and salvation of Jesus to enter heaven! All one must do is to never sin in thought or in deed. If you can honestly make that claim, you are in!

All other religions offer merely, at best, a qualified promise of salvation based on behavior requirements. Followers of them have no guarantee or promise of eternal life with God.

Jesus did everything that He could do to get you! Now it's up to you to choose whether you will accept Him. As you consider your options, consider these thoughts:

If you believe that death is a benign dirt nap, what have you to lose by giving your life to Jesus? What would the cost to you be?

If you are an atheist or agnostic, are you really willing to bet eternity in hell that you are right? If you are of another religion, which seems more likely to offer you the highest probability of eternal salvation, your religion or the gospel of Jesus?

Whatever you decide, keep reading! It's never too late to rethink your position.

If anyone or anything including yourself makes you feel less than, never forget the price Jesus paid for you. You are worth the life of God Himself.

YOU ARE GOD'S GLORIOUS INHERITANCE.

3

Jesus Gave Us His Grace

GRACE IS GOD'S WILLINGNESS, ABILITY, AND POWER THAT HAS DONE THOSE THINGS FOR US THAT WE CANNOT OR WILL NOT DO FOR OURSELVES.

From now on, when you hear or read the word *GRACE*, go back and read this definition until you have it memorized. Defining grace as God's unmerited favor is akin to calling a Lamborghini a cup holder.

When God put on a flesh suit and walked the earth under the name Jesus, He ushered in or brought with Him a new covenant. You may have heard that term and wondered what it meant.

Allow me to explain. This new covenant, which basically means new deal, was between Himself in the person of God and Himself in the person of Jesus. The covenant was not between man and God, but between God and God, thus making it unbreakable by either party. The new deal or new covenant is an entirely new program of our/man's relationship with God.

Simply put, God freed the Jews from a performance or works or behavior-based relationship where things had to be earned from Him to a relationship of GRACE, as defined above.

Gentiles, which includes everyone not born as a Jew, were without hope and lost in the world. Yet, they did have a path to salvation—Grace. If a gentile sought God with all of their heart and served him and lived a pure life, one that was based on pleasing God, they would be saved. Just as with the Jews, the gentile's relationship with God was based on performance and use of human faith.

Think of the new covenant being an honor system. God had faith that we will accept Him and change our behavior without having to make us behave grudgingly or out of necessity or by threat of punishment.

Here is how the disciple John who wrote five books of the Bible put it:

For while the law (the impossible to keep ten commandments and 603 attached made by men ordinances) was given through Moses, GRACE AND TRUTH came through Jesus. (John 1: 17)

When God chose to leave His throne in Heaven to come rescue His inheritance, (fill in your name), He didn't do it impulsively.

As you read in the chapter on salvation, they had a very real problem. Their children, the ones that they created to live in a state of GRACE with, rebelled against them.

You can't even imagine how wonderful the world that God created for Adam and Eve was. They moved at the speed of thought. Anything they wanted was theirs without asking. They were given dominion and authority over everything in their world. They walked in the cool of the evening with God, literally. The place where they lived was paradise. It truly was a garden of Eden.

Then they got conned into committing sin by the evil one posing as a snake. The unwanted growth, as God calls him, convinced Eve then Adam that God was holding out on them. He used the same age old taunt that he uses today: "SURELY, He did not say!" The stench isn't smart, but he is persistent and the most excellent and effective of all conmen and liars. His favorite tactic is to call The Word of God into question. It happens every Sunday in churches all over the world.

The stench in God's nostrils goes to church to teach Jesus's children that He did not mean what He said, and that He is holding out on them. Satan's goal is to convince Jesus's flock that they must do things to earn the stuff that God is withholding from them—like obey rules, get more faith, expand their faith, keep the Hebrew law, be good, pray hard, pray in groups, beg God, and hope that he is in a good mood.

The world was awash in sin and by their own choosing. God's people placed themselves under a set of impossible to keep laws. So they were separated from God in all of His Forms. Because God cherishes and cannot do without those that He creates, something had to be done.

Here is a dissertation given to Paul, our appointed teacher, by the Holy Spirit:

Just as in His love, He chose us in Jesus actually selected us as individuals for Himself, as His own before the foundation of the world, so that we would be holy and blameless in His sight; IN LOVE.

Our new plan of salvation was instituted as an act of love. Note that God/Jesus/The Holy Spirit/The Word, selected YOU for Himself before He created this planet. Our loving Daddy brought the new program of grace and truth into the world so that we could live with Him forever. He put us in a grace relationship/covenant with Him because He cherishes us so much.

He predestined and lovingly planned for us to be adopted to Himself as His own children THROUGH JESUS, in accordance with the KIND INTENTION AND GOOD pleasure of His will- to the praise of HIS GLORIOUS GRACE and FAVOR, which He so FREELY bestowed on us in the Beloved, His Son Jesus (Ephesians 1:4–6).

Once He selected YOU, He had to find a way to make you free from sin in His sight. How? BY HIS GLORIOUS GRACE.

That was it! His glorious and kindly intended GRACE would make YOU free from sin through the intentional sacrifice of the only being worthy of entrance into heaven, the only being without sin.

BY HIS GLORIOUS GRACE, God sacrificed Himself in the person of Jesus and paid, through horrid punishment, the cost of our sins COMPLETELY, ONCE AND FOR ALL.

And in accordance with this will of God, we have been made holy, consecrated, and sanctified through the offering ONCE, FOR ALL Of the body of Jesus (Hebrews 10:10).

Asking God to forgive us is nonsense! It is not possible for God to forgive us more than He did on the cross. The same is true for healing. It was by this Grace that God was able to forgive us.

IN HIM (Jesus), we have redemption [that is, our deliverance and salvation] through HIS (Jesus) BLOOD, [which paid the penalty for our sin and resulted in the forgiveness and COMPLETE pardon of our sin, in accordance with the riches of HIS GRACE. WHICH HE LAVISHED ON US. IN ALL WISDOM AND UNDERSTANDING WITH PRACTICAL INSIGHT (Ephesians 1:4–8).

Pay attention to that last verse. God's Grace-based plan for our redemption was not an impulsive decision! He developed His salvation plan "In All Wisdom And Understanding, With Practical Insight."

It is not written, but I believe that God prayed that no sin would enter the world, and because of that, we would all live in grace and truth and perfection. God chose to give man freewill. He hoped that men would behave well out of their love of doing good. Yet, the first humans instead used their freewill to commit sin.

Now that same freewill is the root of all wrong. God does not do evil. God does not allow evil. Men do that. Men kill, Men steal, Men destroy, aided and abetted by the butt boil scratch; and his lies, are what cause the disasters that men blame God for.

PLEASE read slowly and thoroughly word for word the first chapter of Ephesians. There is power and joy in that chapter. Among many other blessings, you will learn that you have the same power operating in you that raised Jesus from the dead. You will also learn that YOU are God's glorious inheritance.

God needs nothing except YOU! Just as you learn that you are what God gets, you will learn that you also get a wonderful inheritance. You will learn about this predestination business. You will learn that God predestined YOU to belong to Him.

PLEASE shower yourself with the indescribable love of God. Not based on your behavior, but based on His enormous, infinite, gracious, merciful, joyous, peace filled, happy and, above all, LOVING heart.

Some chuckle headed teachers explain to people who have not been successful in life that God predestined them to be failures. Yes, they do! That is not what predestination is about.

Some clergy actually tell people who are gravely ill that they were predestined to die at a young age. It's sad but true.

Here is what Predestination means: GOD'S WILL FOR YOU!

Folk frequently tell me that they have no idea what God's will for them is. You just read God's will for you. Here it is:

JUST AS IN HIS LOVE, HE CHOSE US IN JESUS. HE ACTUALLY SELECTED US FOR HIMSELF AS HIS OWN BEFORE THE FOUNDATION OF THE WORLD SO THAT WE WOULD BE HOLY AND BLAMELESS IN HIS SIGHT. IN LOVE, HE PREDESTINED AND LOVINGLY PLANNED FOR US TO BE ADOPTED TO HIMSELF AS HIS OWN CHILDREN, THROUGH JESUS IN ACCORDANCE WITH THE KIND AND GOOD PLEASURE OF HIS WILL, TO THE PRAISE OF HIS GLORIOUS GRACE AND FAVOR WHICH HE SO FREELY BESTOWED ON US IN THE BELOVED JESUS (Ephesians 1:4–6).

I purposely reported this scripture twice, because it is so important! Now you know God's will for YOU and every human being on this planet.

HOW HE DID IT

Now you know that God's will for us is that we become His children forever and ever. Also learn His plan for accomplishing that goal:

"BUT GOD—so rich is He in His MERCY! Because of and in order to satisfy the great and wonderful and intense love with which He loved us, even when we were dead by our own shortcomings and trespasses, He made us alive together in fellowship and in union with Jesus; [He gave us the very life of Jesus Himself, the same new life with which He made Jesus alive] for it is by GRACE that you are saved (delivered from judgment and made partakers of Jesus's salvation.)

"And He raised us up together with Him and made us sit down together giving us joint seating with Him in the heavenly sphere by virtue of our being in Jesus."He did this that He might clearly demonstrate through the ages to come the immeasurable limitless, surpassing riches of His free grace in Kindness and goodness of heart toward us in Jesus.

"FOR IT IS BY FREE GRACE THAT YOU ARE SAVED (delivered from judgment and made partakers of Jesus's salvation (which is a free gift received on acceptance of Jesus. At that moment, we get Jesus's faith.) THROUGH FAITH."

Write down this definition of *faith*, and memorize it:

FAITH IS THE SUBSTANCE FORMED BY LIVING NOW IN THIS PRESENT MOMENT, WITH JOYFUL EXPECTATION, OF THE THINGS THAT WE CANNOT SEE, BUT HAVE BEEN PROMISED BY THE HOLY SPIRIT. (Hebrews 11:1)

Everybody has some notion of what they think faith is. The one above is the only definition of faith in the Bible. Since the Holy Spirit who wrote the Bible is the ultimate expert on faith, I choose to accept His definition.

AND THIS SALVATION IS NOT OF YOURSELVES BUT IS THE GIFT FROM GOD: NOT BECAUSE OF WORKS [Not the fulfillment of the Law's demands], LEST ANY MAN SHOULD BOAST. *[It is not the result of what anyone can possibly do, so no one can pride himself in it or take glory to himself].* (Ephesians 2:4–9)

So why all the caps and underlining and big letters and italics? Because this is the plan for Your/Our salvation.

If you want to know what the most important scriptures in the Bible are, they are John 3:16, Romans 10:10, and what you just read. Not only are these scriptures urgent for our salvation, they teach us the true nature of our relationship with our eternal King. They teach us how infinite His love for us is. They teach us that God not only loves YOU and I infinitely, but that He took action based on that love.

He did something for us that no other could or would. He gave us the greatest gift of all time: Eternal Life. Regardless of what you may have heard or read, there are no other qualifications than to believe in our hearts that God raised Jesus from the dead, and to confess with our mouths that He is our King.

Is that surprising? So many are confused by current teaching. If the teaching you are hearing does not agree with these words, don't listen—RUN!

4

Jesus Gave Us His Peace

Let be and be still, and know that I am God! (Psalm 46:10)

This is a teaching directed to those who have an honest desire for relief. It is especially given to those who need rest and hope.

If you find yourself in a frequent state of stress, tension, pessimism, nervousness, anxiousness, depression or fear; if you feel that nothing ever goes right for you; if you just want to give up, and you are constantly tired, this Word is for you.

Jesus knows you in a very deep and personal way. He wants to minister to you right where you are, even as you read this epistle. That is why you are reading this book. It is not by chance, but by His plan.

Jesus knowing that the people of His time knew nothing of biology or the unseen world of atoms and molecules and cells, made a pronouncement that they could understand:

Are not five sparrows sold for two pennies? And not one of them is forgotten or uncared for in the presence of God. *But even the hairs on your head are all numbered. Do not be struck with fear or seized with alarm you are worth more than many flocks of sparrows.* (Luke 12:6–7)

If we had been His audience with the knowledge we now possess, Jesus would have taught us that every one of our hundreds of trillions of cells are numbered, and that He lives within them and their sub cells to infinity.

Here is a message directed to all mankind. It was given to the prophet Isaiah to deliver to the children of Israel and to all of humanity by God in the person of the Holy Spirit. It describes what happened when God came to earth in the person of Jesus!

The people who walked in darkness have seen a great Light; those who dwelt in the land of intense darkness and the shadow of death, upon them has the Light shined. You, O Lord, have multiplied the nation and increased their joy; they rejoice before You like the joy in harvest, as men rejoice when they divide the spoils of battle, for the yoke of Israel's burden and the staff or rod for goading their shoulders, the rod of their oppressor, You have broken as in the day of Gideon with Midian. For every tampering warrior's war boots and all his armor in the battle tumult and every garment rolled in blood shall be burned as fuel for the fire. For to us a Child is born, to us a Son is given; and the government shall be upon His shoulder, and His name shall be called Wonderful Counselor, Mighty God, Everlasting Father of Eternity, PRINCE OF PEACE. Of the increase of His government and PEACE there shall be no end! (Isaiah 9:2–6)

The yoke of Israel's burden are the 603 ordinances they made up and the Ten Commandments, which the Jews brought upon themselves by rejecting God. They soon discovered that they were impossible to keep.

Jesus Bought Us Perfect Peace

I love this teaching from Jesus! In it he expressed His desire for all of humanity to have PERFECT PEACE. Check it out:

"But take notice the hour is coming and it has arrived, when you will all be dispersed and scattered, every man to his own home, leaving Me alone. Yet I am not alone. because My Father is with Me. *I have told you these things, so that in Me you may have PERFECT PEACE and confidence. In the world you have tribulation and trials and distresses and frustrations; but be of GOOD cheer! For I have overcome the world."* (John 16:33)

This is a promise of perfect peace from our King. Yes, in this world, we will be buffeted, attacked, spoken ill of, and we will find tribulation.

BUT be of GOOD cheer! Be Happy and Joyful and Excited and Expectant of Victory! Because no weapon of any kind can prosper against you! Because Jesus has overcome whatever the trial in your life is for you!

Again, a prophetic message to us personally from our Daddy God in the person of the Holy Spirit:

But no weapon that is forged against you shall prosper, and every voice that shall rise against you in judgement you shall show to be wrong."This PEACE, righteousness, security, triumph over opposition is the heritage of the servants of the Lord; this is the righteousness or the vindication which they obtain from Me,"says the Lord. (Isaiah 54:17)

This is a guarantee from God Himself. It is for those who accept Jesus as their King. No one need guess what that means. It is implanted in us to serve our precious Lord.

The Lord God in the person of the Holy Spirit downloaded to another prophet, Micah, the coming of Jesus. Micah did his best to report the great and joyful news to the children of Israel:

NOW GATHER yourself in troops, O daughter of troops, a state of siege has been placed against us, They shall smite the ruler of Israel with a rod on the cheek. But you, Bethlehem you are little to be among the clans of Judah; Yet out of you shall One come forth for Me Who is to be the Ruler in Israel. Whose goings forth have been from of old, from ancient days, (eternity) therefore shall He give them up until the time that she who travails has brought forth; then what is left of His brothers shall return to the children of Israel. And He shall stand and feed His flock in the strength of the Lord, in the majesty of the name of the Lord His God; and they shall dwell secure, for then shall He be great even to the ends of the earth. And this one SHALL BE OUR PEACE, when the Assyrian comes into our land and treads upon our soil and in our palaces, then will we raise against him seven shepherds and eight princes among men. (Micah 5:1–5)

This is a very important prophecy. It is one of the more than 400 specific prophecies about Jesus that were fulfilled in His life.

It essentially calls for Israel to protect herself from the coming invaders. It warns that they will come and denigrate Jerusalem and its worldly leaders. It reveals that for a time, Israel will be defeated, while it's judges and leaders will be wounded.

It promises that regardless of these negative events, the promised one—the Messiah—will come, and that He will come from of all places little Bethlehem, a lowly crossroads village of absolutely no import. It declares that the Messiah has been for eternity and will be forevermore, and that He will rule over all of His people, and no army or enemy can prevail against them. For that reason, He is our everlasting peace!

GREAT NEWS

Here again is our anointed teacher, Paul, writing a summary of why and How Jesus is the Prince of Peace:

But now in Jesus, you who once were so far away, through the blood of Jesus have been brought near. For He is Himself OUR PEACE, our bond of unity and harmony. He has made us both Jew and Gentile one body, and has broken down (destroyed, abolished) the hostile dividing wall between us, by abolishing in His own crucified body the Law with its decrees and ordinances (the 603 manmade ordinances and the 10 commandments) *WHICH HE ANNULED; that He from the two, might create in Himself one new man, one new quality of humanity out of the two (Jews and Gentiles which is everybody) so making PEACE. And He designed to reconcile to God both Jew and Gentile united in a single body by means of the cross, thereby killing the mutual enmity and bringing the feud to an end. And He came and preached the glad tidings of PEACE to you who were afar off and PEACE to those who were near. For it is through Him that we both now have an introduction, access by one Holy Spirit to the Father so that We are able to approach Him.* (Ephesians 2:13–18)

This is the GREAT NEWS of the Gospel of Jesus!

We who were far away from God, because of our sins, have been given one hundred percent totally complete forgiveness of all of our sins—past, present, and future. And because of that forgiveness, we have also been given access to Him through Jesus.

Our sins are no more because of the blood of Jesus. Jesus abolished the system of having to be good. He fulfilled the Ten Commandments which were the barrier to the Jews from God. He wiped out the sins of the Gentiles.

Jesus purchased our PEACE with His blood!

Again, the prophetic message dictated to the prophet Isaiah by the Holy Spirit to be delivered to all mankind:

Surely He has borne our griefs (Maladies, sicknesses, illnesses and diseases) *and carried our sorrows and pains of punishment, yet we ignorantly considered Him stricken, smitten and afflicted by God as if with leprosy. But He was wounded for our transgressions, He was bruised for our guilt and iniquities; the chastisement* (punishment) *needed to obtain PEACE and well-being for us was upon Him and with the stripes* (from the whip with strands tipped with rocks and pieces of bones, he felt the excruciating pain from all forty lashes) *that wounded Him we are healed and made whole.* (Isaiah 53:4–5)

If you want everlasting peace around the clock, just accept Jesus. Is that a deal? Ask yourself what receiving the love, peace, grace, mercy, eternal salvation, and joy would cost you. Ask yourself if you are willing to gamble your eternal life on being right.

This is another beautiful promise to us from God in the Person of the Holy Spirit, written by Paul:

REJOICE *(RE-JOY-YOURSELF. CHOOSE TO LIVE IN JOY AND HAPPINESS)* in the Lord always (*delight, gladden yourselves in Him*) again I say, Rejoice! Let all men know and perceive and recognize your unselfishness your considerateness, your forbearing spirit. The Lord is near. DO NOT FRET OR HAVE ANY ANXIETY ABOUT ANYTHING, but in every circumstance and in everything, by prayer and petition, with thanksgiving in your heart, make your wants known to God.

This statement seems to contradict the fact that Jesus has already given us everything. No, Paul wrote this to the Hebrews who had not yet accepted Jesus and all of His great and precious promises.

Here comes the HUGE DEAL . . .

AND GOD'S PEACE WHICH TRANSCENDS ALL UNDERSTANDING SHALL garrison and mount guard over your hearts and minds IN JESUS (Hebrews 4:6–7)

Explanation: When we do not fret or be anxious about anything or any circumstance, but trust Jesus and praise Him and give Him Thanks, we in return gain the PEACE THAT TRANSCENDS ALL UNDERSTANDING.

My Partner, friend, and cofounder of Throne of Grace Ministries, Mr. C., uses the word *PEACE* as an exclamation point! I'm not sure he even realizes it, but it blesses me every time he says it.

Why? Because it reminds me that Peace is not only attainable, it is a free gift from our King. In all of my years in ministry, the number one thing that I have learned that people seek is PEACE. Put another way, probably more accurately, they want the byproduct of peace: relief!

CAST YOUR EYES UPON JESUS

There is an old protestant hymn which goes as follows:

Cast your eyes upon Jesus,
Look straight in His glorious face
and the cares of this world will grow strangely dim
in the light of His glory and grace.

Those beautiful words pretty much sum it up.

One day, many years ago, I was on a ministry/business trip
with my friend, Carlos. It was very close to Christmas time,
my favorite season of all. Carlos and I sat on a bench in
La Jolla, California, in a shoreline park. The park is located
right on the ocean between the cove and the kids pool. So
beautiful!

Carlos and I were expressing our gratitude, admiration, and
love for our Daddy God and our King Jesus. We discussed
several scriptures. As we did, a true peace hung over us.

As we talked about Jesus, night fell and the stars became
visible. Then the most beautiful purple sky appeared. It was
so gorgeous! I felt that I was looking directly into the face of
King Jesus! Instantly, all of my cares seemed to melt away,
and I felt His presence.

As I soaked in the glory of my Lord and Savior, I knew that
He had His arms around me, hugging me and telling me to
enter into His rest. I could hear His voice saying:

*"And pay attention! I Am with you all the days, perpetually,
uniformly and on every occasion, to the very close and
consumption of the age, so let it be!"* Matthew 28:2

Those words make me shudder each time I read or hear them! I take them as a personal message to me. I hear Jesus telling me to be at peace and know that He is always with and in me FOREVER. No Words or thought give me more peace and comfort.

Jesus actually gave us a precise prescription or formula to gain and maintain peace at all times. In this message, Jesus presumes that we understand that there is no time in God's lexicon. Time is a man-created measuring device that has no relevance in His World:

DO NOT WORRY!

Therefore, I tell you, stop being perpetually uneasy, anxious and worried about your life, what you shall eat or what you shall drink or about your body, what you shall put on. Is not life greater in quality than food, and the body far above and more excellent than clothing? Look at the birds of the air; they neither sow nor reap nor gather into barns, and yet your heavenly Father keeps feeding them. Are you not worth much more than they? And who of you by worry and being anxious can add one unit of measure to his stature or to the span of his life? And why should you be anxious about clothes? Consider the lilies of the field and learn thoroughly how they grow; They neither toil nor spin. Yet I tell you, even Solomon in all his magnificence, excellence, dignity and grace was not decked out like one of these! But if God so clothes the grass of the field, which today is alive and green and tomorrow is tossed into the furnace, will He not much more surely clothe you, O you of little faith? Therefore, do not worry and be anxious, saying, "What are we going to have to eat? or What are we going to have to wear?" For the Gentiles the Heathens (Those who do not know or care about God/Jesus/The Holy Spirit. Or those who today purposely reject them) *wish for and crave and diligently, seek all these things, and your heavenly Father knows well that you need them all.*

Jesus commanded us not to worry or be anxious about anything, because He has given us all things that pertain to life and Godliness. Instead of worrying and begging Jesus to do that which He has already done, we need expect and receive His gifts by speaking them into existence, celebrating our receipt of the things that He gave us by grace, through using His faith, which He gave us as a free gift.

The Gentiles (heathens, unbelievers, worshippers of false Gods) have to worry, beg, plead, struggle for these things by whatever means at their disposal, because they do not know or accept Jesus.

"But seek, aim at strive after first of all His kingdom and His righteousness (Jesus) and then all these things taken together will be given you besides."

When you lock on to Jesus with all of your heart, when you treasure Him and the Words of the Holy Spirit above all other things, you will know the truth, and the truth will make you free!

The truth, the only real truth, is the Gospel of Jesus! The truth is that you have already been given everything you seek!

So do not worry or be anxious about tomorrow, for tomorrow will have worries and anxieties of its own. Sufficient for each day is its own trouble. (Matthew 6:25–34)

Once, a man came to me for help. The man was eaten up with worry, depression, gloom, despair, self-condemnation, guilt, and shame. Nobody, and I mean nobody, could stand to be around him for more than a minute; woe be to those who made the horrid mistake of asking him how he was. The result was a tirade of self-pity. People ran and hid from him.

I had several meetings and teachings with the poor soul to no avail. I could stand it no more! I told the dude that if he wanted me to continue to try and help him, he must read Matthew 6:25–34 out loud until he had it memorized, then recite it ten times a day for at least thirty days. When he felt that he understood why we gave him the assignment, he was to call us for an appointment to discuss the teaching.

Forty-one days after, I received his call and agreed to meet with him for lunch. I was flabbergasted at the change that came over "Negative Ned."

He was happy, full of joy, excited, and on fire for Jesus! Everybody, and I mean everybody, couldn't get enough of him. His conversations were always about the person he was with and Jesus.

Negative Ned had transformed into Positive Pete! Pete was so happily married to the Holy Spirit that he sold his business, and he attended Andrew Womack's Charisma Bible College and moved to India with his son.

Today, those two fine Spirit-Led Jesus Lovers lead many churches in India that they started. I forgot to mention that they converted from Judaism to Christianity.

DO NOT WORRY!

"Do not worry" is a direct command to us from Jesus. If you are a commandment thumper, here is one from our King! We must live in this present moment and not seek knowledge of the future. The fruit of the tree of knowledge caused sin to enter the world.

Jesus only operates and lives in this present moment. He was infinitely, He is infinitely, and He will be infinitely. Thus the present is all that exists. His formula for peace is simple yet difficult. We are reliant on our concept of time.

To achieve living in the present, you must practice strenuously until you have let go of the past and the future. Amazingly, Albert Einstein spent his entire life trying to define time. He failed miserably.

The best he could do was to posit a theory that energy equals mass times the speed of light squared, which is a presumption based on the theory that a second is a second.

The Holy Spirit explained time to us through the wisdom that He gave King Solomon, in one minute.

That *which has been (the past) is now; (the present) and that which is to be (the future) has already been; (past) and God requires that which is past.* (Ecclesiastes 3:15)

There it is! BOOM! All time is the same in God's world. There is no time in God's or our lives. Try to touch the past or the future or move in them using your senses. Impossible, because they do not exist.

Are you beating yourself because of your past? Do you beg God to forgive you for an act you committed in the past? Do you dwell on the past or the future or talk to God about either? When you do, God has no idea what you are talking about!

Jesus wants us to move into His realm, which is the present, so that we can absorb all of Him.

THE THREE THEATERS

One day, many years ago, I asked the Holy Spirit how I could best teach my flock how to live in the present. Following is the analogy that He gave me. It has helped many people:

THE PAST

Imagine yourself enjoying a nice walk down the street on a lovely day. You come upon a beautiful theatre. On the marquee are written these words: THE PAST, STARRING (fill in your name); and in little tiny type, these words: "written, produced, and directed by the father of all lies."

You are mesmerized by your name appearing on the marquee, and you miss the small print and rush in. On your way in, you are given delicious refreshments and flowers. You are beyond excited to see the production.

The film begins, and for the next hour you are glued to your seat while you watch every evil thing you have ever done or thought or spoken. You are tormented by seeing all of the things that you messed up or broke or destroyed in your entire life.

Every sin that you have ever committed in thought or in deed is on full display for you and all to see. You cry, you sob, but you are stuck to your seat and forced to watch. You cannot escape and you can't close your eyes or cover your ears. Your arms are stuck to the seat. The pain is suffocating!

Finally, as your devastation is complete and you are loosed, you run away as fast as you can. In your haste to escape the pain, you run right past another theatre and do not even see it. Soon you are heavily struck by the presence of another theatre.

THE FUTURE

This theatre is so stunning that its beauty takes your breath away. Outside is a barker (an arcane word that means a man who accosts people, pleads with them, and compels them to enter the show. They were prominent at circuses).

"Hi yah, Hi yah, Hi yah, folks, step right in, see the yak woman juggle monkeys on her nose!" An example of their work.

This time the barker barks, "Hi Yah, Hi Yah, Hi Yah, step right in, get a free two-pound lobster dinner and champagne! See the Future starring (fill in your name).

Again there is a huge marquee with your name on it. It reads: The Future Starring You. Once again you miss the small print: "written, produced, and directed by satan."

You are tantalized by the glamour, hoping for a much happier movie! Again you are glued to your seat and are completely immobile.

The movie begins and astonishingly, it is more of a train wreck than the first movie. The entire show is about how horrid your future will be as it is entirely predicated on your failures, sins, and blunders of the past.

You are brainwashed and spirit-washed to believe that as loathsome as was your past, your future will be exponentially worse.

All of your shortcomings that fed your failures are there on the screen following you into tomorrow. The agony is unbearable! Your pain is excruciating. All hope for a better life to come has been squashed forever. You are convinced that you are doomed to repeat the horrors of the past.

The Future you see is predicated on your past as shown in the first theatre. Your mistakes, sins, and failures will be the foundation of your life going forward.

You might as well give up. You couldn't succeed then, and you cannot succeed now! You are quickly convinced that there is nothing you can do to improve your prognosis.

The producer, who is the most skilled con-artist and liar ever, had you in full agreement with his message of doom and gloom. You slink away, morose and heartbroken, filled with gloom, despair, and agony. As you muddle along on your way home, you notice a theatre between the first two.

THE PRESENT

Again, your name is on the marquee. This time it is grander and more splendid. The theatre is much more glamorous than the others. It looks as though it belongs in heaven. You see beautiful lights and colors. You even think you see angels.

You are escorted in by people more loving and caring than any you have ever encountered. Love heavily cloaks the place. You are filled with contentment. The heavenly ushers have wiped your tears away.

You have no need for refreshments. A feeling of compete joy and comfort that you have never before known overwhelms you. You have never felt this much peace and happiness and calm before.

The film begins. Instantly, your eyes are filled with beautiful tears of joy. On the screen are Jesus and you. He tells you how deeply He loves and cares for you in Words so full of harmony and peace and grace that the angels weep tears of great love and gladness for you.

Jesus holds you warmly and tightly. He tells you that you are His True love. He teaches you that he has no scorecard to hold against you.

He tells you that anything that happened before that moment no longer exists in any form. He tells you that the future is a theory, it does not exist.

Our wonderful King tells you that He cherishes you and will always love and protect you. He tells you that you are blessed and highly favored. He tells you that He will always be there with and for you, because you are His!

The love you feel convinces you for the first time that there is unconditional love, and only our Master can gift us with it.

You intuitively know that Jesus is where you should have gone to find love all along. Guilt, Fear, Worry, Anxiety, Self Judgement, Pain, and all negative emotions evaporate, because now you know the truth!

There is no fear, only peace. There are no bills. There is no urgency. There is nowhere to go more compelling than the place where you are.

Here in this perfect place of peace, you find all of the wonderful, great, and precious promises of Jesus come true. Now for the first time, you can see everything that you have been given and you are overwhelmed.

The blinders on your eyes fall off. You can see the heaven on earth that God has prepared for you, and you know how to get and stay there from now on and forevermore.

There is nothing that must be done immediately. There are no social pressures. You and the world are at ease.

You know that you are neither judged nor condemned; rather, you are God's precious inheritance, and you are His most highly valued possession.

You want to stay forever and ever, and you can. It is your choice. Sadly, most ignore the present moment that you have just experienced. They urgently rush from the past to the future and back. Everything in their lives is more important than spending valuable and precious time with the Prince of Peace.

They never experience what you just did, because they have no time or energy to stop and go to God's home. So they have no peace.

"Peace I give you; My own peace I now give and bequeath to you. Not as the world gives do I give to you. Do not let your hearts be troubled, neither let them be afraid." (John 14:26–27)

PEACE, LIKE FAITH, IS A FREE GIFT!

The world gives only temporarily. It frequently takes back what it gives. WHEN JESUS GIVES, IT IS A COMPLETE AND PERMANENT GIFT.

Once Jesus gives us a gift, as He did His Faith, it is given in full and cannot be taken away. It cannot be increased, multiplied, divided or subtracted.

Jesus's gifts cannot be stolen, lost or diminished. JESUS GAVE US HIS PEACE, ONCE AND FOREVER. It is our choice to accept His peace by living in the Spirit or reject it by living in the flesh.

In this scripture, Jesus clearly distinguished the difference between how He gives and has given, and how the world gives. His giving is not based on earnings or merit, but on Grace, Mercy, Love, and the sacrificial death that He in the person of the Triune God suffered for us.

RECEIVE THE PEACE OF JESUS IN YOUR SPIRIT! ENTER INTO HIS REST!

When that Peace invades our Spirit, we should be bursting with joy every day and showing it. We should be walking around, singing joy songs like "IN THE GARDEN" all day.

As my dear friend, Teacher Ron Reeser says, we should go about our daily lives "Beaming Love To Everyone."

Please receive the peace that our dear Lord gave you. He loves you so dearly! He paid such an awful price to give you peace. It's yours for the taking!

5

Jesus Gave Us His Mercy

King David, led by the Holy Spirit, wrote these accurate words about God's MERCY:

O GIVE thanks to the Lord, for He is good; for His mercy and loving-kindness endure forever.

O give thanks to the God of gods; for His mercy and loving-kindness endure forever.

O give thanks to the Lord of lords for His mercy and loving-kindness endure forever.

To Him Who by wisdom and understanding made the heavens, for His mercy and loving Kindness endure forever,

To Him who made the great lights, for His mercy and loving-kindness endure forever.

To Him Who stretched out the earth upon the waters, for His mercy and loving-kindness endure forever.

To Him Who made the great lights, for HIs mercy and loving-kindness endure forever. (Psalm 136)

David's praise song about the mercy of God continues for twenty-six verses. You may ask what made David such an expert on the mercy and loving-kindness of Jesus. Practical Experience. David was a murderer, a peeping tom, an adulterer, and a liar. Yet, God forgave his sins and called David a man after God's own heart.

Paul, under the direction of the Holy Spirit, wrote these beautiful words about the mercy and grace of God:

Inasmuch then as we have a great High Priest Who has already ascended and passed through the heavens, Jesus the Son of God, let us hold fast to our confession of faith in Him; for we do not have a High Priest who is unable to understand and sympathize and have a shared feeling with our weaknesses and infirmities and liability to the assaults of temptation, but One Who has been tempted in every respect as we are, yet without sinning. Let us then fearlessly and confidently and boldly draw near to the THRONE OF GRACE, that we may RECEIVE MERCY for our failures and find grace to help in a time of need. (Hebrews 4:14–16)

It is important to understand that our God is full of mercy, grace, and love for us as individuals. He dotes on us, regardless of our behavior. He certainly does not appreciate our sins, but He keeps no record of them. In fact, GOD HAS NO MEMORY OR RECOLLECTION OF OUR SINS!

"The Lord Your God is in the midst of you, a Mighty One, a Savior Who Saves! He will rejoice over you with joy; He will rest in silent satisfaction and in His LOVE He will be silent and make no mention of past sins or even recall them: He will exult over you with singing." (Zephaniah 3:17)

YES! GOD HAS NO RECOLLECTION OF OUR SINS AFTER WE ACCEPT THE SALVATION OF JESUS.

THE REAL GOD

Here is the real God who was Jesus in the flesh. The Jews refused to listen to God. So God spoke to them through prophets who listened to Him, received His Word and repeated that Word to the people. The people were sinning like crazy and then offering sacrifices to atone for their wickedness. God gave them a message of rebuke through the prophet Hosea:

"For I desired Mercy and not sacrifice; and the knowledge of God more than burnt offerings." (Hosea 6:6)

Clearly, God meant that He would rather have had His children demonstrate charity, kindness, and mercy to their fellow man, and for them to seek and therefore know Him, rather than to make offerings in atonement. This is a direct message to us about how highly God honors MERCY.

Moses was the first prophet. He was led by the Holy Spirit to write these Words about our loving Father way back in the day:

When you are in tribulation (having horrible problems) and all these things come upon you, in the latter days (now) you will turn to the Lord your God and be obedient to His voice.""FOR THE LORD YOUR GOD IS A MERCIFUL GOD; He will not fail you or destroy you or forget the covenant of your fathers, which He swore to them.* (Deuteronomy 4:30–31)

THE NATURE OF JESUS

Here, in His own words, is how Jesus rolls:

*There was a man who had two sons; And the younger
of them said to his father, Father, give me the part of
the property that falls to me. And he divided the estate
between them.*

*And not many days after that, the younger son gathered up
all the money he had and journeyed into a distant country,
and there he wasted his fortune in reckless and loose
living.*

*And when he had spent all he had, a mighty famine came
upon that country, and he began to fall behind and be in
lack and want.*

*So he went and forced himself upon one of the citizens
of that country, who sent him into his fields to feed hogs.
And he would gladly have fed on and filled his belly with
the carob pods that the hogs were eating but they could
not satisfy his hunger and nobody gave him anything.
Then when he came to himself, he said, "How many hired
servants of my father have enough food, and even food to
spare, but I am perishing here of hunger!"*

*I will get up and go to my father, and I will say to him,
"Father, I have sinned against heaven and in your sight, I
am no longer worthy to be called your son; just make me
like one of your hired servants."*

*So he got up and came to his own father. But while he was
still a long way off, his father saw him and was moved with
pity and tenderness for him; and he ran and embraced
him and kissed him fervently.*

And the son said to him, "Father, I have sinned against heaven and in your sight; I am no longer worthy to be called your son."

But the father said to his bond servants, "Bring quickly the best robe, the festive robe of honor and put it on him; and give him a ring for his hand and sandals for his feet."

Please note that the Father—who represents God/Jesus/ The Holy Spirit/The Word—did not even hear, much less pay attention to, the sons confession of sin! So it is with us and God.

This is also a great teaching about confession and repentance. Pay attention to the fact that the Father did not give one thought to the boy's confession. What was important to the father was that the boy returned to Him.

Jesus is the same way. When we stop sinning and rejecting Him, and return to Him, all of the heavenly host celebrate and kill the fatted calf.

"And bring out that wheat fattened calf and kill it; and let us revel and feast and be happy and make merry, because this my son was dead and is alive again; he was lost and is found!" And they began to revel and feast and make merry.

The irresponsible son is us before we accept Jesus. When the boy returned to his Father, he was like us when we come to Jesus.

Our sins have been washed away by the blood of Jesus. God has no recollection of them. He is not interested in sin! God only wants you/us to fall madly in love with Him and to return to Him by making Jesus our king.

Now comes the other brother who is all about keeping rules and regulations and being sinless. He is very angry that the father didn't throw his brother out on his ear. He is enraged about the party.

The older brother is a type of religious folks today. The old works-based "fuddy-duddys" cannot stand the "grace message." They are the "holier than thou" crowd. They like to judge others. They are in for a very rude surprise.

The day is coming when they will learn that they have no greater position with God than the riotous living son who returned.

But his older son was in the field; and as he returned and came near the house, he heard music and dancing. And having called one of the servant boys to him, he began to ask what this meant.

And he said to him, "Your brother has come, and your father has killed that fattened calf, because he has received him back safe and well."

But the elder brother was angry with deep seated wrath and resolved not to go in. Then his father came out and began to plead with him.

But he answered his father, "Look! These many years I have served you, and I have never disobeyed your command. Yet you never gave me so much as a little lamb that I might revel and feast and be happy and make merry with my friends; but when this son of yours arrived, who has devoured your estate with immoral women, you have killed for him that fattened calf."

*And the father said to him, "Son you are always with me,
and all that is mine is yours. But it was fitting to make merry,
to revel and feast and rejoice, for this brother of yours
was dead and is alive again! He was lost and is found!"*
(Luke 15-32)

Many anti-organized religion folk complain about the
hypocrites in churches. My opinion is that this is largely an
excuse. However, there certainly are hypocrites in church.

The older brother represents them. He is a type of those
who sit smugly in their bought and paid-for pew in the
first church of high holiness. They sit in judgement and
condemnation of "sinners." You would be surprised to know
how many calls I get from people who are concerned about
sister or brother so and so. "Pastor Allen, I am gravely
concerned about brother Pigsniffel."

These folk actually believe that they are greater in the
kingdom than newcomers or brother Pigsniffel. Have you
friends of Bill Wilson ever seen a drunk homeless guy show
up at an AA meeting? The righteous indignation of the
assembled is stunning.

Yes, they are saved, and as Jesus proclaimed, they have
always had all that is His, even though they don't know or
believe it. They "walked the aisle" when they were seven
years old, and have never missed a Sunday since.

Now they cringe when a prostitute or thief or someone who
stinks shows up.

HOW JESUS ROLLS

The Pharisees and Scribes and Sadducees who were the
spiritual leaders of the Jews in Jesus's day were out to

kill Him. They had several serious conundrums. The Jews were subject to the Roman Government. It was against the Roman Law for a Jew to execute another Jew, no matter who it was that was bringing charges.

So the Jews were always trying to trap Jesus or trick Him into committing a crime that was punishable by death under the Roman law. They tried several of these, and all had failed. This time, they thought they had a humdinger. They just knew they had Jesus in a "When did you stop beating your wife?" trap.

Here is how it went down. They went out and caught a woman in the act of adultery. The 603 man created ordinances required such a woman be stoned to death. The Roman law said that it was a capital offense to stone another Jew.

The plan was to get Jesus to break one or the other law. When He did, they would have a capital crime to prosecute Jesus with. Problem solved!

Read what Jesus did:

BUT JESUS went to the Mount of Olives. Early in the morning, He came back to the temple court, and the people came to Him in crowds. He sat down and was teaching them, when the scribes and Pharisees brought a woman who had been caught in adultery. They made her stand in the middle of the court and put the case before Him.

"Teacher," they said, "This woman has been caught in the very act of adultery. "Now Moses in the Law commanded us that such women offenders shall be stoned to death. But what do You say to do with her—what is your sentence?"

They said this to test Him, hoping they might find a charge on which to accuse Him. But Jesus stooped and wrote on the ground with His finger.

However, when they persisted with their question, He raised Himself up and said, "LET HIM WHO IS WITHOUT SIN AMONG YOU THROW THE FIRST STONE AT HER." Then He bent down and went on writing on the ground with His finger.

They listened to Him, and then they began going out, conscience-stricken, one by one, from the oldest down to the last one of them until Jesus was left alone, with the woman standing there before Him in the center of the court.

When Jesus raised Himself up, He said to her, "Woman, where are your accusers? Has no man condemned you?"

She answered, "No one, Lord!"

And Jesus said, "I do not condemn you either. Go on your way and from now on sin no more." (John 8:1–11)

I believe that Jesus wrote each person's sins in the sand. When they looked down, they saw all of their sins. That is why they dropped their stones. They knew that Jesus was God, because He had written down their personal sins known only to them and God.

IT IS URGENT to understand this: there was only one person who was qualified to cast a stone at the woman— Jesus! Not only so, but Jesus was required by the Hebrew Law to stone the woman to death. Jesus broke the Law in favor of MERCY!

LORD HAVE MERCY!

I have heard this statement or request all of my life. It puzzles me how it ever came to be. Jesus is Mercy. Jesus is the definition of Mercy. He bought our freedom from punishment by being beaten nearly to death and then crucified.

The chastisement necessary for our peace was upon Him. (Isaiah 53:5)

Our King paid the price for our sins! How could you have more mercy than that? Here is a message from our King about what happens to those who are shown mercy, yet do not practice mercy:

THE MERCILESS SERVANT

Therefore the Kingdom of Heaven is like a human king who wished to settle accounts with his attendants.

When he began the accounting, one was brought to him who owed him 10,000 talents (*probably about 10 million dollars*).

And because he could not pay, his master ordered him to be sold with his wife and his children and everything that he possessed, and payment to be made.

So the attendant fell on his knees, begging him, "Have patience with me and I will pay you everything."

And his master's heart was moved with compassion, and he released him, cancelling the debt.

But that same attendant, as he went out, found one of his fellow attendants who owed him a hundred denarii (about twenty dollars); and he caught him by the throat and said, "Pay what you owe!"

So his fellow attendant fell down and begged him earnestly, "Give me time, and I will pay you all!"

But he was unwilling, and he went out and had him put in prison till he should pay the debt.

When his fellow attendants saw what had happened, they were greatly distressed, and told everything that had taken place to the master.

Then his master called him and said to him, "You contemptible and wicked attendant! I forgave and cancelled all that great debt of yours because you begged me. And should you not have had pity and mercy on your fellow attendant as I had pity and mercy on you?"

And in his wrath, his master turned him over to the torturers (*the jailers*) till he should pay all that he owed.

So also My heavenly Father will deal with every one of you if you do not freely forgive your brother from your heart his offenses. (Matthew 18:23–35)

There are so many lessons and messages in this teaching that are easily missed. Obviously, the teaching is about forgiveness.

It's about God's forgiveness being a demonstration of how deep and sincere and complete our forgiveness should be, because he completely forgave us.

This parable teaches us that God has freely and completely forgiven us all of our sins as a product of His great love and mercy. Therefore, we must freely, and from the heart, forgive those who have trespassed against us; that is only our reasonable service.

As God has shown us complete and total Mercy, we must treat others with pity and mercy. The teaching is about how highly God values the quality of mercy and the depth of which He has forgiven us.

JESUS IS MERCY!

6

Jesus Gave Us The Holy Spirit

Most people, even those who have known Jesus for a very long time and have attended church for many years, know nothing of the Holy Spirit.

They have heard of Him, but they have no idea who He is, where He came from, what He does or what His purpose is. Some think of Him as an ethereal Ghost, because He is often referred to as the Holy Ghost.

Let's clear up some questions about The Holy Spirit:

The Holy Spirit/Holy Ghost is God in Spirit form. The Holy Spirit, Jesus, and our Daddy God are all in one and one in all.

That concept is not as difficult as folk make it. My car has seats. My car has a stereo. My car has an engine. They perform different functions, but they are all my car.

Each of the Members of the Triune God, play urgent roles. Jesus was God in the flesh! The Holy Spirit is God in Spirit form. All three created everything that is.

All three hold everything that is together. Each of them lead with LOVE! All three parts of God are the pulsating illuminating energy (LIGHT) that holds everything together and in place. All three are in the minutest infinite sub particles of matter. That is precisely why matter cannot be destroyed.

In the beginning was the Word, and the Word was with God, and the Word was God. The same was with God in the beginning. All things were made by Him; and without Him was not anything made that was made. In Him was life; and the life was the LIGHT of men! (John 1:1–3)

Without Their congealing power to stabilize opposing and equal forces, the universes unto infinity would explode.

Each of them are required to maintain all things that are. God as all three persons—God, Jesus, and The Holy Spirit—are the force that created all things and maintain all things, hold them together, and make them possible.

If the earth were one billionth of a degree off course, we would all cease to be. More importantly, if any force in all of space were out of place by the most infinitesimal fraction, nothing would exist.

Jesus went to heaven to return to His throne as King of Kings, but stayed here with us to protect and guide us in the person of the Holy Spirit.

THE PROMISE OF THE HOLY SPIRIT!

Here is how Jesus opened His comments about the Holy Spirit:

"IF YOU LOVE ME, YOU WILL KEEP MY COMMANDS. AND I WILL ASK THE FATHER AND HE WILL SEND YOU ANOTHER Counselor. Helper, Intercessor, Advocate, Strengthener and Standby, that He may remain with you forever—The Spirit of Truth. Whom the world cannot receive because it does not see Him or know Him, but you Know and recognize Him for He lives with you constantly and will be in you. I will not leave you as orphans, comfortless, desolate, bereaved, forlorn, Helpless; I will come back to you."(John 14:15–18)

JESUS SPOKE OF HIS COMMANDMENTS, NOT THE TEN COMMANDMENTS OF MOSES!

You learned about the commandments of Jesus in an earlier chapter. Let's take another look at them. As you review the commands of Jesus, note how much easier and lighter they are than the law of Moses. Remember that unlike the commandments of the Hebrews, Jesus's commands are voluntary. It is important to understand that keeping Jesus's commands is a demonstration of our love for Him. Keeping Jesus's commands brings joy, peace, and happiness to us, to others, and to Jesus.

As you continue in this book, you will see how Jesus repeatedly proved His love for us. You will fall in love with Jesus. When you fall in love with Jesus, keeping His requests is natural and easy.

THE COMMANDMENTS OF JESUS

Jesus declared that His yoke is light and His burden is easy. Here is a representative sample. Check them out:

I consider this to be the first and most important commandment of Jesus. He had just taught the Jews who were astonished by His Word that He was the replacement for the commandments and laws. They freaked out and asked Jesus this question:

Then they said, "What are we to do to carry out what God requires of us?"

Jesus replied, *"This is the work that God asks of you: that you believe on the One Whom He has sent!"* (John 6:29)

This next command is so important! Jesus lives in the present. He has no use for the past or future. The past no longer exists, and the future is unknown.

He teaches that if we want to know peace, we must live with Him in the moment. All of Gods treasures and blessings are ours in the moment. There is no need for worrying in this present moment. This present moment is a primary component of faith.

Here is a very important commandment of Jesus:

"DO NOT WORRY! Therefore, I tell you, stop being perpetually uneasy, anxious, worried about your life, what you shall eat or what you shall drink; or about your body, what you shall put on. Is not life greater in quality than food, and the body than clothing?"

Here is Jesus's commandment to live in this present moment:

"So do not worry or be anxious about tomorrow, for tomorrow will have worries and anxieties of its own. Sufficient for each day is its own trouble." (Matthew 6:34)

This commandment is a one hundred percent Guarantee from the Creator of all things:

"Seek first the Kingdom of God and His righteousness and these things shall be yours and more." (Matthew 6:33)

This just means to pursue Jesus with all of your heart. It means to desire Him above all things. By the time you finish this book, you will know why and how.

The next commandment of Jesus is for our physical and spiritual health. It is the most potent medicine in existence. If you are stressed take this pill three times a day:

"Do not let your hearts be worried, you believe in God, believe also in Me!" (John 14:1)

This commandment is a call to surrender. It is an order for us to let go of our struggles and stresses and heaviness, and give them to the one who wants to carry them for us.

"Come to me all of you who labor and are weighed down heavily, learn of me, for my yoke is light and my burdens are easy." (Matthew 11:28)

We have all heard of the golden rule. It is true about every act we commit toward our brothers and sisters. It is also true about giving. When you are considering an offering or a tip for a person who performs a service for you, remember this commandment. It will serve you well:

"Do unto others as you would have them do unto you." (Luke 6:11)

This is one of Jesus's final commandments, and it is very important to Him. It is by our love for each other that men will know us as lovers of Jesus.

"Love each other as I have loved you! Love your neighbor as you love yourself!" (John 13:34)

Remember the original promise? "If you love me you will keep MY COMMANDS, and I will ask the Father and He will send you another, a Comforter."

In contrast to the easy commands of Jesus are the impossible to keep Commandments given to the children of Israel who rejected God. Try this on for size:

"Hear, O Israel, The Lord our God is One Lord; And you shall love the Lord your God out of and with your whole heart and out of and with all your soul, your life, and out of and with all your mind with your faculty of thought and your moral understanding, and out of and with all of your strength" (Mark 12:30)

That is the first of the ten commandments of Moses. It was given to Moses to show how impossible it would be for anybody to keep Laws well enough to earn salvation or right standing with Him.

Study Jesus and learn His commandments!

MORE EXCELLENT NEWS ABOUT THE HOLY SPIRIT

However, I am telling you nothing but the truth when I say it is profitable for you that I go away. Because if I do not go away, the Comforter, Counselor, Helper, Advocate, Intercessor, Strengthened Standby will not come to you;

into close fellowship with you; but if I go away, I will send Him to you.

And when He comes, He will convince the world and bring demonstration to it about sin and about righteousness, uprightness of heart and right standing with God and about judgement:

About sin, because they do not believe in Me; About righteousness because I go to My Father, and you will see Me no longer; and judgement because the ruler *[satan]* of this world is judged and condemned and sentence is passed upon him.

I have many things to say to you, but you are not able to bear them or to take them upon you or to grasp them now. But when He the Spirit of Truth comes, He will guide you into all truth. For He will not speak His own message (*on His own authority*) but He will tell whatever He hears from the Father;

He will give the message that has been given to Him and He will announce and declare to you the things that are to come. He will honor and glorify Me, because He will take of what is Mine and will reveal it to you. (John 16:7–14)

HOW COOL IS THAT?

Wouldn't you like to have the Holy Spirit whisper to you what the truth is in every situation and show you all the things that are going to happen, in advance?

The evidence of accepting Jesus, obeying His commandments, is being "Reborn." That means to have a fundamental change in our way of life brought on by a sincere desire to be like our loving Daddy and to please Him.

Food for thought. Not everyone who is saved has been reborn. I see "believers" every day that haven't changed one bit since they "walked the aisle." In fact, they are worse than ever.

Before you call a person a "Born-Again Believer," consider what being born again means.

WHAT BEING REBORN LOOKS LIKE

So this I say and solemnly testify in the name of the Lord as in His presence, that you must no longer live as the heathen (those who have rejected Jesus) do in their perverseness, in the folly, vanity and emptiness of their souls and the futility of their minds.

In their spiritual apathy they have become callous and past feeling and reckless and have abandoned themselves a prey to unbridled sensuality, eager and greedy to indulge in every form of impurity that their depraved desires may suggest and demand. But you did not so learn Jesus!

Assuming that you have really heard Him and been taught by Him as all Truth is in Jesus embodied and personified in Him.

Strip yourselves of your former nature put off, discard your old un-renewed self which characterized you through lusts and desires that spring from delusion; And be constantly renewed in the spirit of your mind having a fresh mental and spiritual attitude And put on the new nature the regenerate self-created in God's image, in true righteousness and holiness. (Ephesians 4:17–24)

HAVE YOU BEEN BORN ANEW?

Being born anew means to live in the Spirit. It means to have a Spiritual awakening. It means having your eyes and your mind solidly locked into the unseen world of God. It means to release the cares of this world. It means to make God/Jesus/The Holy Spirit the most important thing in your life; not lip service, but for real and certain. Being born again is an absolutely voluntary action. It can never be achieved grudgingly or by coercion or by guilt or fear of punishment. It only comes through the love of Jesus.

Before we can love Jesus or anyone else, we need to learn to love ourselves. This is a requirement before we can give love back to another.

Loving Jesus is so easy when you learn how He feels about you.

JESUS TEACHES ABOUT A NEW LIFE

Here is a teaching from Jesus about being led of the Holy Spirit and being born anew. It happened like this:

A Pharisee who knew for a fact that Jesus was God in the flesh was horrified of the cost to him of being caught with Him. He slithered out to see The King of Kings at night!

He knew that he was putting his entire life at stake. If caught, he would lose his multimillion-dollar job. There are some like this today.

In today's world, he could lose his 40 million dollar salary. His books might not sell. His flock might leave him. He might lose his financial engine or worse, his 25 million dollar mansion.

He might lose his social status. The cool folk might eject him from their clique. Worse, he might be forced to sell his jet or Lamborghini.

This priest named Nicodemus, like the leaders of today's church, knew that there might even be the possibility of losing his membership at the Blue Nose Country Club. So old Nick prayed that none of his group would hear or see that he had been there.

Instead of falling on his knees before Jesus in public, in broad daylight, and asking His forgiveness and making a declaration of his willingness to abandon all to follow and serve God, he had the audacity to call him "Rabbi/ Teacher."

Jesus was not a Rabbi! He was God in the flesh and this man, swollen with pride, knew it. It was an insult to Jesus to call Him teacher.

Read the incomprehensible foolishness of his comments:

"Now there was a certain man among the Pharisees named Nicodemus, a ruler, a leader, and authority, among the Jews,"Who came to Jesus at night and said to Him. "Rabbi, we know and are certain that You have come from God as a Teacher; for no one can do these signs (these wonder works, these miracles— and produce the proofs) that You do unless God is with him."

Ya Think, Nick?

Jesus answered him, "I assure you, most solemnly I tell you, that unless a person is born again he cannot ever see the kingdom of God."

The answer appears to be unrelated to the question. Here is what it means:

Nicodemus was incapable of understanding or acknowledging who Jesus was, because he had no spiritual vision. He was entirely submitted to the seen world around him. He had no spiritual discernment. He only knew that Jesus was God based on what he saw. He saw Jesus fulfilling the known prophecies about the Messiah. His heart and ears were, however, closed to the Spirit of God. His heart was hardened.

He was completely under the control of his flesh and the deception of satan. He was frozen by the fear of loss. Please understand this: Jesus is not saying that you cannot enter heaven without being born again. If He were, there would only be a few "believers" in heaven.

Jesus meant exactly what He said. If you want to SEE the kingdom of God, you must be born again as written about above.

We are given the opportunity to walk in God's Kingdom while we are still on earth. We walk into heaven when we accept and choose to believe Jesus.

We have been given the power to have spiritual eyes and vision. With them, we can actually see the Kingdom of God. To see the kingdom, we must have our spiritual eyes open.

Now we are reduced to an even lower state of intellect. Stupidity squared! This is without qualification the most inane, vapid, void of mind, hammer headed, mentally numb question ever asked!

Nicodemus said to Him, "How can a man be born again when he is old? Can he enter his mother's womb again and be born?"

Jesus answered, "I assure you, most solemnly I tell you, unless a man is born of water and The Spirit, he cannot ever enter the kingdom of God."

This time Jesus does mean that you cannot ENTER heaven unless you have been born of water and the Spirit. Entirely different truth.

Being born of the water is not what some folk believe that you must be water baptized to enter heaven.

When Jesus refers to being born of water, He means to be born the natural way, as in when a Mothers water breaks. When He speaks of being born of the Spirit, He means that in order to accept Jesus and make Him your King and thus be saved, you must be led by the Holy Spirit.

Jesus meant precisely what He said. Unless you accept Him as your Savior, because you must be saved, there is no way to enter into heaven.

Jesus continued:

"What is born of/from the flesh is flesh, and what is born of the Spirit, is Spirit. Marvel not, do not be surprised or astonished at My telling you. You must be born anew. The wind blows, breathes where it wishes, and though you hear its sound, yet you neither know where it comes from nor where it is going. So it is with everyone who is born of the Spirit."

This teaching seems very strange and incomprehensible. In fact, it is very simple. We know that the wind exists because we can see its effects. We can feel the wind, but we cannot see it.

A person born of the Spirit is renewed and changed, and believes differently and behaves differently. We can't see the Holy Spirit changing the person, but we know that he has.

A side note: Jesus always spoke in irrefutable logic. One may deny, obfuscate, ignore or refuse to believe Jesus, but no one may accurately deny the pure logic of His Words.

We may determine the direction and speed of the prevailing winds in an area; however, no matter how sophisticated the tech world gets, they will never be able to determine where wind originates or ends.

Back to the Spiritually-blind Pharisee:

"Nicodemus answered by asking, "How can all this be possible?"

Jesus replied, "Are you the teacher of Israel, and yet do not know nor understand these things? Are they strange to you?"

"I assure you, most solemnly I tell you, We speak only of what we know. We know absolutely what we are talking about! We have actually seen what we are testifying to."

"And still you do not receive our testimony!

You reject and refuse our evidence—that of Myself and of all those who are born of the Spirit! If I have told you of things that happen right here on the earth and yet none of you believes Me, how can you believe if I tell you of heavenly things?" (John 3:1–12)

Jesus was referring to all of the miracles signs and wonders that He had performed. The Pharisees knew that Jesus had raised the dead at least four times, healed every disease known to man, turned water into wine, fed 15,000 people with five loaves of bread and two small fish, and many more signs. Yet they rejected Him. They refused to believe that He was the Messiah.

There are so many lessons in these few Words of Jesus. Nicodemus was willing to throw away eternal life to avoid the consequences of acknowledging Jesus. We laugh at the spiritual idiocy of old Nick, but does the fear of what others think of us not drive many of our behaviors and beliefs as well?

There will be people who read and agree with every bit of the content of this book who, out of fear of what others will think, would rather die than share it with a friend, neighbor, relative or fellow worker.

LIFE IN THE SPIRIT

Therefore, there is now no condemnation no adjudging guilty of wrong for those who are in Jesus, who will live and walk not after the dictates of the flesh, but after the dictates of the Spirit. For the law of the Spirit of Life which is in Jesus has freed me from the law of sin and death. (Romans 8:1–2)

Here is more from Paul about how Jesus fulfilled the law and ordinances, and in doing so, freed the Jews to live a life in the Spirit. It is also about life in the Spirit for us as well.

"For God has done what the Law could not do, it's power being weakened by the flesh [the entire nature of man without the Holy Spirit]. Sending His own Son (Himself in the flesh) God condemned sin in the flesh [subdued, overcame, deprived it of its power over all who accept the sacrifice." (Romans 8:3)

God did so by walking the earth and being tempted at all points, yet not sinning, and thereby fulfilling the entirety of the commandments and ordinances for the Jews who were under the law and, entirely incapable of doing so.

So that the righteous and just requirement of the Law might be FULLY MET in us who live and move not in the ways of the flesh but in the ways of the Spirit (our lives governed not by the standards and according to the dictates of the flesh, but controlled by the Holy Spirit).

For those who are according to the flesh and are controlled by its unholy desires, set their minds on and pursue those things which gratify the flesh, but those who are according to the Spirit and are controlled by the desires of the Spirit set their minds on and seek those things which gratify the Holy Spirit. Now the mind of the flesh; which is sense and reason without the Holy Spirit is death, that death that comprises all the miseries arising from sin, both here and in the hereafter. But the mind of the Holy Spirit is life and soul peace both now and forever.

That is because the mind of the flesh with its carnal thoughts and purposes is hostile to God, for it does not submit itself to God's laws; indeed, it cannot.

So then those who are living the life of the flesh, catering to the appetites and impulses of their carnal nature cannot please or satisfy God or be acceptable to Him.

But you are not living the life of the flesh, you are living the life of the Spirit, if the Holy Spirit of God really dwells within you (directs and controls you). But if anyone does not possess the Holy Spirit of Jesus, he is none of His (he does not belong to Jesus, is not truly a child of God).

But if Jesus lives in you then although your natural body is dead by reason of sin and guilt, your spirit is alive because of the righteousness that He imputes to you.

And if the Spirit of Him Who raised up Jesus from the dead dwells in you, then He Who raised up Jesus from the dead will also restore to life your mortal, short lived, perishable bodies through His Spirit Who dwells in you.

So then, brothers, we are debtors, but not to the flesh we are not obligated to our carnal nature, to live a life ruled by the standards set up by the dictates of the flesh.

For if you live according to the dictates of the flesh, you will surely die. But if through the power of the Holy Spirit you are habitually putting to death, making extinct, deadening the evil deeds prompted by the body, you shall really and genuinely live forever.

For all who are led by the Spirit of God are sons of God.

For the Spirit which you have now received is not a spirit of slavery to put you once more in bondage to fear, but you have received the Spirit of adoption (the Spirit producing sonship) in the joy and happiness and bliss of which we cry,"Abba Father! Father!"(Romans 8:4–15)

The essence of what you just read is this: when you give your life to Jesus completely, meaning that you are willing to follow Him and His way of life, you receive the Holy Spirit.

When you receive the Holy Spirit, you are led by Him and you change. You are no longer controlled by the part of you that wants to rebel against God and goodness. Rather, you are controlled by the Holy Spirit who will help you see what is right, guide you, and help you do right things.

"WE CRY, "ABBA FATHER!"

Meaning Daddy, Daddy! When we are led by the Holy Spirit, we fall in love with our precious Daddy and we cry out to Him, overwhelmed with our desire to be with Him!

Do you remember when your kids would run to you, and jump in your arms, and say, "Daddy, Daddy!" So it is with those of us who are led by the Spirit.

The Holy Spirit attests to us how amazing, loving, glorious, happy, kind, generous, caring, peaceful, forgiving, and joyous our Daddy God is!

The Spirit Himself thus testifies together with our own spirit, assuring us that we are children of God. And if we are His children, then we are His heirs also: heirs of God and fellow heirs with Jesus sharing His inheritance with Him; only we must share His suffering if we are to share his glory. (Romans 8:7–17)

What Paul means by "suffering" is the sacrifice of our flesh-led minds. It means that if we wish to be joint heirs with Jesus, we follow His lead and live not by the flesh but by the Holy Spirit. He does not mean that we are supposed to suffer physically, mentally or spiritually.

Some very foolish folk have wrongly interpreted this teaching that it is in God's plan for us to suffer! No, really, they have. Have you ever seen the post on Facebook that claims that Jesus has a purpose for our suffering and pain?

Suffering with Jesus means to live with the attacks and abuse and loss of prestige, bullying, and social rejection that are the consequences of telling people—especially religious people—that you believe that every single word of the Bible is true and inerrant.

Suffering with Jesus means to fight to put down our flesh and be good and speak truth, and do things that please our Father, instead of being led of the flesh to do what is wrong. Remember, Jesus was tempted at all points as we are, but He fought His flesh and did not sin.

Suffering with Jesus means to be persecuted for not going along with the crowd and following traditional beliefs. Jesus destroyed tradition and paid the price of being scorned because He wanted the approval of His Father, not the approval of His friends.

THE MEANING OF LIVING IN THE FLESH

We are spirits that live in physical bodies that have souls. The soul is the mind and heart realm. Our flesh lives in the soul realm.

The flesh is the opposite of the Spirit. It is the stubborn, rock-hard rebellious part of our souls. The flesh demands to see physical evidence before it chooses to believe. The flesh demands control, and rejects any kind of authority or behavior modification.

The flesh demands evidence of anything that can't be seen with the natural eye. The flesh rejects the things of God in exchange for immediate self-gratification.

The flesh is that self-centered childish part of us that is narcissistic. It insists on getting what it wants when it wants it. It stomps its feet like an aggravated three-year-old in a toy store.

The flesh is full of competition, bigotry, prejudice, self-pity, self judgement, condemnation, anger, bitterness, meanness, vengeance, "smart-assed-ness," sarcasm, ego, satisfaction, superiority, score keeping, conceits, judgement, arrogance, and the insistence on being right.

The flesh believes that it has no need for God, because it thinks that it is in control. It, in fact, insists on being in control.

The flesh enjoys this world and is bound to it. It will often cling to this life even after the spirit has left it. Inordinate fear of dying is evidence that one is led of the flesh.

The flesh believes itself to be superior in intellect and moral authority to an unseen God. It has a better program than God. The rebellious self-demands that it makes the rules.

Grasp this teaching that is completely contradictory to the behavior of the flesh, from Paul:

For we cast our eyes not on the things which are seen, but on the things which are unseen. For the things that are seen are temporary and subject to change. The things that are not seen are of God and are eternal. (2 Corinthians 4:18)

Look at what Paul tells us is the behavior that comes from living in the flesh:

But I say walk and live habitually in the Holy Spirit responsive to and controlled and guided by the Spirit; then you will certainly not gratify the cravings and desires of the flesh, of human nature without God.

For the desires of the flesh are opposed to the Holy Spirit, and the desires of the Spirit are opposed to the flesh (Godless human nature); *for these are antagonistic to each other, constantly fighting and in conflict with each other, so that you are not free but are prevented from doing what you desire to do.*

But if you are guided by the Holy Spirit, you are not subject to the Law.

THE DOINGS OF THE FLESH

Now the doings, practices of the flesh are clearly obvious: they are immorality, impurity, indecency idolatry selfishness, divisions, dissensions, party spirit factions, sects with peculiar opinions, heresies, Envy, drunkenness, carousing, and the like. I warn you beforehand, just as I did previously, that those who do such things shall not inherit the Kingdom of God. (Galatians 5:19)

That last scripture is so easily misunderstood. Paul is NOT writing about followers of Jesus. He is writing about those who reject Jesus and live a life of sin doing these behaviors as a lifestyle.

Those who live like that clearly have not accepted Jesus. Jesus's people live in a state of Grace. Our sins are forgiven once and for all—past, present, and future.

Until the moment of death, even murderers—including abortionists who have committed the greatest genocide ever perpetuated on earth—if they are sincere and are willing to accept Jesus as their King, can be saved.

DO NOT GAMBLE. DO NOT BELIEVE THAT YOU CAN JUST LIVE LIKE HELL AND THEN WAIT UNTIL THE LAST MOMENT TO ACCEPT JESUS! YOU CAN'T ACCURATELY PREDICT WHEN THAT MOMENT WILL BE!

Sadly, I had a dear friend who fell down dead from a cerebral hemorrhage at the age of forty-three! Never saw it coming. Had he not long ago accepted Jesus, He would be cracking and popping.

My grandfather died of a mustard gas induced heart attack at the age of forty-two. Same deal. My Uncle got killed instantly in a horrible drunk driving accident at the age of thirty-one. John F. Kennedy never expected to die that day in Dallas. Do not wait to accept Jesus.

When Paul spoke of unrepentant sinners perishing into a horror-filled eternity, He was not talking about those who are saved and yet sin.

HOW JESUS FOLLOWERS TRY TO LIVE

Again, a beautiful teaching from Paul:

But the fruit of the Holy Spirit the work which His presence within accomplishes is love, joy, gladness, peace, patience, an even temper, tolerance, kindness, goodness, benevolence, faithfulness, gentleness, meekness, teachableness, self-restraint. Against such things there is no law that can bring a charge. And those who belong to Jesus have crucified the flesh (the Godless human nature, with its passions and appetites and desires.

If we live by the Holy Spirit, let us also walk by the Spirit. If by the Holy Spirit we have our life in God, let us go forward walking in line, our conduct controlled by the Spirit, let us not become vainglorious and self-conceited, competitive and challenging and provoking and irritating to one another, envying and jealous of one another. (Galatians 5:20–25)

The fruits of the Spirit are not easy to employ. They require willingness to change. They require effort. Changing is an action, not just a thought. Walking in the Spirit is the most wonderful feeling possible.

Try this: when you are bound and determined that you must lie to a person to cover up or deny wrongdoing or for any other reason, STOP, take a deep breath, and say to yourself, "I am a follower and lover of Jesus! I am going to tell the truth no matter what!" Then do it and reap the reward of the wonderful feeling that comes from honesty.

That is, of course, unless as they say in AA, "To Do So Would Injure Yourself Or Others." In only very few cases is this true. It means something like admitting to a long affair that has long since been ended.

Try blessing others and/or a Church or Ministry. Make an unscheduled and unsolicited financial gift to a person or group in need. Feel the wonderful effect of helping others. Swallow your pride and apologize for a wrongful act that you committed against another. Freely, and purely with the help of the Holy Spirit, forgive someone. Make a decision to stop fighting. Allow a person to pass you in traffic or let another driver merge in front of you.

Stop wasting your time worrying about politics and world events. All you can do is vote, speak your thoughts, and support your candidate. You cannot change results.

Over-tip a waitress, Bless a Vet, Thank a police officer, Bless a person of opposite opinion from yours. There is no greater feeling than doing good! You cannot possibly experience greater joy, peace, and happiness than when you are led of the Holy Spirit and do something good. Money can never purchase such great happiness.

Hearing Jesus:

Listen to Jesus in the person of the Holy Spirit. He broadcasts constantly. If we don't hear Him, it is because we are not tuned to His frequency. If Jesus Had a radio station, it would be WLOVE or KLOVE. Jesus knows each of us individually and gave everything to prove His love for us. He actually knows You by Your name. GOD, JESUS, HOLY SPIRIT CALLS YOU BY YOUR NAME!

They love to have dialogue with us. Jesus wants us to talk to Him and discuss our issues and problems with Him. To Jesus that means that we trust Him. He loves for us to praise, thank, and glorify Him. He loves to praise and glorify us.

Pretend that you have Jesus following you, carrying you, hugging and loving you all day and night, every day and night; because you do.

The watchman (the Holy Spirit) *opens the door for the shepherd* (Jesus) *and the sheep* (His followers, us) *listen to His voice and pay attention to it; and He calls His own sheep by name and leads them out. When He has brought His own sheep outside, He walks on before them, and the sheep follow Him because they know His voice.*

They will never on any account follow a stranger, but will run away from him because they do not know the voice of strangers or recognize their call. (John 10:3–5)

The sheep that are My own hear and are listening to My voice; and I know them, and they follow Me. And I give them eternal life, and they shall never lose it or perish throughout eternity. (John 10:27)

Those words should bring tears of joy to your eyes. How wonderful is it to know that the Creator of all things hungers after a dialogue with you?

How great is it that our God knows us by name, and we know Him? We know our Lords voice. He knows our voices. I promise you that if you shut down the white noise, turn off the computer, cell phone, etc., and listen, you will hear sweet Jesus call you by your name. You will know that the voice you hear is Jesus, because it will be so kind, gentle, and loving that you know that it is He.

Think about this: Close your earth mind and visualize what you are reading! God loves you so much that The Holy Spirit wrote this book for you personally, and placed it in your precious hands.

Perhaps this is the first time that you have thought about the Holy Spirit. Remember that He is as much a part of God as God is! He is very real, to be revered, and to be accepted and believed, just as God and Jesus are.

7

Jesus Healed Us

YES, HE DID! Asking Jesus to heal you or others is confounding to God! He cannot understand what you are talking about. After you read this chapter you will understand why.

PLEASE DO NOT BE OFFENDED.

THERE IS ABSOLUTELY NOTHING WRONG WITH USING MEDICAL SCIENCE FOR HEALING! GOING TO THE DOCTOR DOES NOT MEAN THAT YOU DON'T BELIEVE JESUS.

The things that Jesus did are stunning to us. They are hard to wrap our modern minds around. We have been entrenched in steadfast unbelief since Jesus returned to His throne. The Author and I simply wish to teach you the promises that are available to you if you can bring yourself to absorb them, believe them without doubt, and speak them into existence.

JESUS HEALED EVERY DISEASE KNOWN AND UNKNOWN TO MAN BY DYING FROM ALL OF THEM ON THE CROSS!

Inevitably, folks, ask this question when I teach on healing: "Well, if that is true, we would never die right?" Let's answer that question up front.

God created us to die. He doesn't want us to live on this planet longer than our designated time, because He can't stand being away from us. Okay?

It's not that we are not going to die. It's a matter of when we die and how. There is no reason for us to be ill or suffer from some disease or die young. Jesus took all sicknesses, illnesses, diseases, maladies, and infirmities into His body on the cross and died from them. He was unrecognizable as a human.

Yes, at the moment He gave up the ghost, He was suffering from all known and unknown diseases. He had AIDS, Alzheimer's, Cancer, STD's, Ms, Md, Cp, COPD, Cirrhosis of the Liver, Diabetes, and every other infirmity. He nailed them all to the cross.

Can you imagine when we go on social media and ask God to heal all people with Cancer, how it makes God shake His head in astonishment? Can you imagine how repulsive this comment is to God? "God Has A Purpose For Your Pain and Suffering!"

Imagine how Jesus feels when His children that He died to heal come to him, begging him, even in groups to heal someone.

THE CULPRITS ARE IGNORANCE AND UNBELIEF

One of my FAQ's is this: If Jesus healed all diseases, why do people get sick? Why do we need hospitals and doctors?

Ignorance of what Jesus did on the cross is very common among the people; yes, even "believers." I have met very few "believers" who know that Jesus destroyed all disease once and for all on the cross. The source of ignorance is the leaders of the church who pass it along for whatever reason.

The problem is not your ignorance-based unbelief, it is the COLLECTIVE UNBELIEF OF HIS CHILDREN!

Here are more FAQs:

Why does God allow children to get bad diseases? Why does He allow cancer to exist? Why did aunt Sally die such a long and horrible death when she believed, had faith, and did not want to die? Why did God heal Elroy down the street, but not Bob next door? Did Elroy have more faith than Bob?

WE ARE ALL PRODUCTS OF OUR EDUCATION.

What we do not know will hurt us. What we insist on that is errant can as well. The evil one has spread all kinds of crazy non-biblical teachings around the body of Jesus. When we receive them as paradigms, they keep us from receiving those great and precious promises that Jesus purchased for us, such as healing.

FALSE HEALING PARADIGMS

Here is a list of the errant beliefs that have been ingrained in our consciences. You read some of them in our chapter on blasting holy cows:

"Healing requires anointing with oil, putting out a fleece, being prayed for by people with more faith, praying in tongues, fasting and the help of Doctors having their hands guided by the good Lord."

"God will not bless a mess."

"God heals some but not all."

"Jesus's healing's only happened while He was on earth."

"You must be righteous before you can receive your healing."

"God has a purpose for your suffering."

"Sometimes it is in God's will that we get sick."

"You must have enough faith to believe for a healing." (If you have made Jesus your King, you have his faith)

"Healing's are rare miracles."

"God will not heal a person with sin in their lives."

"Healing must be in God's will."

"It has to be in God's time."

"Your sickness is because of a sin you committed in the past."

"Only someone with GREAT faith can receive a healing."

OF COURSE NONE OF THESE ARE TRUE! Why? Because Jesus isn't GOING to heal anybody. He healed every living being on the cross. Honestly, there are otherwise excellent Word and Grace teaching ministries that have healing schools to teach their students how to heal a sick person, which is entirely impossible.

HOW HEALING WORKS

Get this picture: a high priest named Jairus risked his job, money, status in the community, and everything he had. He heard about Jesus. He believed in Jesus. His daughter was quickly dying. He acted on his belief and ran to find Jesus.

On the way to Jesus, the professional mourners who were at the house chased Jairus down and told him that his daughter had died. They told him not to bother the Master, because there was nothing He could do, it was too late.

THEY WERE JUST LIKE THE DOUBTERS, UNBELIEVERS, AND NAYSAYERS OF THIS DAY!

Jairus pressed through the throngs that were surrounding Jesus. He was resolute in his faith that Jesus could and would restore his daughter to health if he asked him to.

While Jairus was working his way to Jesus, a woman was also. The woman had an issue of blood for twelve years. She spent ALL of her money on physicians, and there were good ones in that day. They worked with what we now call holistic medicines, herbs and oils, minerals and plants known to help. Yet, she was no better; in fact, she was worse than ever.

The woman also heard about Jesus. She steadfastly believed that if she just touched the hem of his garment, which was a stoning to death offense, she would be healed.

Both of these people heard about Jesus, made a decision to believe in Him, and acted on their belief. Jairus refused not to believe.

This woman fought her way to Jesus and touched the hem of his garment. The act caught Jesus by surprise. He asked His disciples who had touched Him. The woman admitted without fear of punishment that it was she who had touched Jesus. Instead of punishing her for her crime, Jesus said to her, "Take joy, daughter, your faith has made you whole!"

FAITH IS THE SUBSTANCE CREATED BY LIVING IN THIS PRESENT MOMENT WITH JOYFUL EXPECTATION OF THE THINGS THAT WE CANNOT SEE THAT HAVE BEEN PROMISED BY GOD (Hebrews 11:1).

MEANWHILE, Jairus finally pressed in through the crowd and got to Jesus. He knelt before Jesus and told him that his daughter was dying. He told Jesus that even so, he steadfastly believed that if Jesus came to His home and touched his daughter, she would live and not die and proclaim the works of God.

Many of the people laughed and scorned the priest and Jesus, shouting that the girl was dead. Jesus ignored the doubters and told Jairus to take Him to his house.

When they got to the house, Jesus took only Jairus, John, Peter, and James inside. When they saw the girl, the disciples felt it necessary to tell Jesus that the girl was dead. Jesus sent them out of the room. He didn't want the unbelief of the disciples to affect what He was about to do.

Jesus looked at Jairus and his wife, and said, "Only believe, Jairus!" Then Jesus commanded the girl to rise. The little girl rose out of her bed, and Jesus commanded the parents to get her food and drink and to not tell what had happened (Luke 8:40–56).

In fifteen minutes, Jesus performed two miracles by the power of faith, the same thing that unbelievers to this day call "faith healing" by way of decrying it and mocking it.

The woman with the issuance of blood bet her life on her belief. It was a stoning to death offense for a menstruating woman to touch a Rabbi or Priest.

Jairus was a priest. He could have lost all of his money, his position in the community, his job, and his life for seeking Jesus, much less believing in Him.

STEADFAST BELIEF CAUSED BOTH HEALINGS

Let's dig into this healing business: Why do we have disease and hospitals? Read what happened to Jesus who was God in the flesh as reported by Mark in the sixth chapter of his book, verses 1–5.

He went away from there and came to his hometown, and his disciples followed Him. And on the Sabbath. he began to teach in the synagogue, and many who heard Him were astonished, saying, "Where did this man get these things? What is the wisdom given to Him? How are such mighty works done by His hands?"

"Isn't this the carpenter, the son of Mary and brother of James and Joseph and Judas and Simon? And are not his sisters here with us?" And they took offense at Him.

And Jesus said to them, *"A prophet is not without honor except in his hometown and among His relatives and in His own household."*

And He could do no mighty works there, except that He laid His hands on a few sick people and healed

them. AND HE MARVELED AT THEIR UNBELIEF!
(Matthew 13:55-58)

JESUS COULD DO NO MIGHTY MIRACLES IN HIS
OWN HOMETOWN BECAUSE OF THE COLLECTIVE
UNBELIEF OF THE PEOPLE!

There are two reported instances when Jesus marveled.

Marvel is defined as being filled with wonder and
astonishment. One instance was when Jesus marveled at
the belief of the Centurion whose servant was sick. The
other was here in Capernaum where Jesus marveled at the
unbelief of His family and friends.

He is still marveling at the unbelief of those who claim to be
His family and friends. Belief is something that God/Jesus/
Holy Spirit cannot force on their children.

GOD GAVE US ALL FREEWILL.

When a person becomes seriously ill or a house burns
down or a child gets run over by a car or any bad thing
happens, they are rooted in our freewill or the lies of Satan.
Not God's will.

Remember that! It is urgent that you understand:

GOD DOES NOT DO OR ALLOW EVIL!

Jesus could not be more clear and direct about who to
blame for bad things.

*"The thief comes to kill, steal, and destroy. I have come that
they may have life and have it in abundance."* (John 10:10)

When anyone is killed or stolen from or destruction occurs, it is not in the will of God. It is the result of someone listening to the lies of the evil one.

An example would be a person who makes the decision to drive drunk. It is not the Holy Spirit leading them to do that. When the ensuing accident happens and death occurs, it is not in "God's Plan!"

STOP BLAMING GOD! ITS NOT HIS FAULT!

Some Christians blame bad things on God. I never will forget the response from some of them after the massive hurricane Katrina slammed into and nearly destroyed New Orleans. A man told me that God sent that hurricane to wipe out the prostitutes and gamblers in New Orleans.

"Well," I responded, "God is a terrible aim because Bourbon Street barely got scratched." Thousands of people in several states lost their homes, and some lost their lives. A large number of folk were displaced, and God missed.

THE POWER OF FAITH

Imagine what would happen if everyone believed Jesus at the time He walked the earth and up to this day. Imagine what would happen to disease if everybody or at least a majority of His children knew for a fact that it was not possible for illness to exist!

Imagine what could be possible if all Christians believed Jesus without doubt! Disease would not stand a chance! Imagine what would happen if we routinely spoke divine health over ourselves and our loved ones before they got sick.

"Have faith in God. Truly, I (The Great I Am) say to you whoever says to this mountain, Be taken up and thrown into the sea, and does not doubt in his heart, but believes that what he says will come to pass, it will be done for Him." (Mark 11:22–24)

Far too many of God's beloved children are suffering from diseases that they brought on themselves by speaking them into existence without doubt. Have you ever known a person who said, "I think that I am catching the flu," and did not?

JESUS CARRIED ALL OF OUR DISEASES IN HIS BODY ON THE CROSS!

Surely (not maybe or might) He bore (past tense) our griefs, (our maladies, infirmities, diseases and sicknesses) and carried our sorrows. (anything that makes us sorry, mental illnesses and addictions etc.) Yet we considered Him stricken, smitten by God, and afflicted. (In the days when Jews were under the law and all of the attached ordinances, if one failed to keep any of them and did not atone of his sins, he would be afflicted with the curses of the Abrahamic Covenant. So when they saw the horrible tortured and deathly-ill Jesus, they wrongly assumed that he had sinned and was being punished by God.)

But He was wounded for our transgressions (sins) he was crushed for our iniquities; upon Him was the punishment that brought us peace, and with His stripes, WE ARE (present tense) HEALED. (Isaiah 53:4–5)

To be precise, we were healed when he bore our sicknesses in His body. We were forgiven and made righteous, and reconciled to God by His stripes.

Here is the testimony of Peter the disciple who was an eyewitness to all of the events in Jesus's ministry life:

"He Himself bore our sins in His body on the tree that we might die to sin and live in right standing with God. By His wounds you HAVE BEEN (past tense) HEALED." (1 Peter 2:24)

God ain't gonna forgive you or heal you or anybody. He did all of that on the cross. When Jesus gave up his body, He reported to God that, *"IT IS FINISHED."*

He meant those exact Words. It is finished. So when we ask Him to forgive us or heal us, it is a declaration that we do not believe His Word. It is a cold slap in the face to Jesus.

As for the foolishness about, "If it is in His will." It is in His will. Here is an example of the will of God regarding healing:

Jesus went throughout all the cities and villages teaching in their synagogues and proclaiming the Gospel of the Kingdom and HEALING EVERY DISEASE AND EVERY AFFLICTION. (Matthew 9:35)

Ask yourself this question: If it is not God's will that every disease be healed, which He did on the cross, why did He go about while He was on earth, healing every disease?

How do You receive your healing? It's really not very difficult. You entrench yourself in the belief that it is impossible for disease to live in your body, because Jesus destroyed disease.

When you get a symptom, rebuke it! Call BS on your symptoms. Speak to your body and command it to receive the healing. Jesus gave it 2000 years ago, and do not agree with the symptoms.

You have been given complete authority over all of the trillions of cells and sub cells in your body. Command them to rise up and destroy illegal invaders. Your cells listen to you, and they must obey what you tell them.

Scientists look into subatomic particles with electron microscopes, and the particles seem to rearrange themselves when they are being observed as if they can perceive when they are being seen.

Paul was a man of letters. He had no idea about quantum physics or cell life. Yet he heard the Holy Spirit tell him to write these words:

"By faith, we understand that the universe was created by the Word of God, so that what is seen was not *made out of things that are visible!"* (Hebrews 11:3)

These are some of the most profound Words in the Bible. How could Paul, a man who had never seen a microscope or a telescope and knew nothing about science, write such scientific fact? How could he have possibly known?

How could Paul even know that there was such a thing as a universe? Even if you believe that the Bible is an elaborate hoax written by Shakespeare, ask yourself this: how could Shakespeare know that there was such a thing as a universe?

How could a first century lawyer know about cells, atoms or molecules. How could Paul have understood quantum physics? Yet, he did.

How do we speak illness on ourselves? This is how Jesus explained it:

"The upright, honest, intrinsically good man out of the good treasure stored in his heart produces what is upright, and the evil man (one who is evil and those who refuse to believe Jesus) *out of the evil storehouse brings forth that which is evil; for out of the abundance of the heart the mouth speaks."* (Luke 6:45)

When we tie this scripture with (Mark 11:22), this is what we get:

From the overflow of the heart the mouth speaks, and you will have what you say as long as you have no doubt or unbelief in your heart.

So then, if you believe without doubt that you have a disease, and you speak it over yourself, you will have what you say.

The evil one rejoices when we make negative comments or prophecies over ourselves. Those words are touchdowns for the "unwanted growth (old scratch)."

They mean that he has won by leading us to a confession that is contrary to the Word of God. When we do so, we are in agreement with him and not Jesus.

Not believing Jesus is the evil one's great ambition for us. When we doubt Jesus, the burnt up cankerworm scores a touchdown. He goes about doing the only thing he can do—lying to God's folks. He always calls the Word of God into question.

Jesus tells us that Satan goes about as a roaring lion, seeking whom he may devour. Lions don't hunt. They sleep and have sex with the lionesses. The lionesses do the hunting.

In the lion world, the old lions who can't do anything else are placed far away from the pack of lionesses. Their job is to roar loudly and scare the unsuspecting victims into running away from him, right into the lionesses.
The evil one has no power in our lives unless we give him power. His big lie is that he is all powerful. In fact, the only weapon he has is to lie.

Old scratch is the father of all lies! He is proficient at lying. He is stupid, but he is very tenacious and persistent and patient. He tries his best to convince the children of God that God's Word could not possibly be true.

Think about this whopper that he has sold: when that child got run over by the garbage truck, it was in "God's Plan."

If you disagree that the burnt up worm is stupid, ask yourself this question: what idiot would start a rebellion against God?

DO NOT ASK UNBELIEVERS TO PRAY FOR YOU

If you want to walk in divine health, NEVER ask people who do not believe the Gospel of Jesus to pray for you. All that the prayer of unbelief accomplishes is to cast aspersions on God. Few "believers" believe Jesus!

Instead, make a decision to believe beyond a shadow of a doubt that you were healed by Jesus on the cross, then behave as if you have been healed.

If you knew in advance that your medical report would be that you walk in total health, you would be extremely happy and grateful. You would celebrate, and you would share the good news with all of your friends and family. Do that.

Don't wait for the confirmation of men. Celebrate!

There is power in unity. If you want others to pray with you, make sure that they are in truthful belief with you in your healing. If they are, this happens:

"Again, I tell you, if two of you on earth agree (harmonize together, make a symphony together) *about whatever* (anything and everything) *they may ask, it will come to pass and be done for them by My Father in heaven. For wherever two or three are gathered, drawn together as My followers in My name, there I AM in the midst of them."* (Matthew 18:18–19)

TESTIMONIES

I guess the reason it is so easy for the Author and I to know for a fact that Jesus has healed all, is by the many healings' that we have personally seen people receive, by speaking healing over themselves through steadfastly believing Jesus.

They are healed by using the faith of Jesus which He freely gave them. Not by laying on of hands or anointing oil, but by believing Jesus. Allow me to share just a couple of them with you. I hope they encourage you! My friend, Mr. B., and I were called to the bedside of a man diagnosed with stage-4 cancer. His doctors were about to release him after his last surgery. They sent him home to die. They told his wife to summon the hospice people as quickly as she could. They told her that he would be dead in a few days.

Mr. B. and I didn't pray for our friend, Mr. E. We sat with him for an hour and explained the Gospel of Jesus regarding healing. When we finished, Mr. E. was in complete agreement with Jesus that he was healed by Jesus on the Cross.

That was five years ago. Mr. E. has side effects from what the doctors did to him, but he has not had one single cancer cell in his body since then. He is healthy as a horse, and we use him constantly to bring hope to others who have been told to die.

THE SAILOR

Nearly twenty years ago, a friend came to me and told me that his uncle had been diagnosed with stage-4 cancer that had spread throughout his body. The cancer, they said, was in all of his organs. In addition, his liver was shot, and his heart was operating at less than thirty percent capacity. He had been sent home to die as well. The doctors proclaimed that it was just a matter of a few days, and at most a few weeks, before his imminent demise.

The partners of Throne of Grace Ministries made the man a beautiful prayer blanket, which is a symbol of our belief that the recipient is healed. We spoke in agreement that he had been healed and commanded all of his good cells to rise up and destroy the rebellious cells.

We explained the Gospel of Jesus to him, and the man came into agreement with Jesus that he was healed. The man's greatest hope was that he would live to see his grandson be born.

The man lived to play with his grandson for six more years before he passed of a heart attack.

His family buried him with his prayer blanket which was emblazoned with the seal of the United States Navy. They said that he carried the blanket with him at all times up until the moment he passed.

MR. JOE

Mr. Joe was a wonderful and very funny man. He was my neighbors Dad. Mr. Joe had played for the Chicago Cubs back in the day. He had a million stories.

Mr. Joe, came to visit his daughter, my neighbor, about once every three months. When he came, he would park a folding chair in her driveway, and sit and enjoy the sun, and chat with her neighbors.

Every time I drove by on my way home and saw him sitting in his chair, I would stop and just listen to him talk for hours. I came to love visiting with old Joe.

One day, I saw him and stopped and asked him how he was. Now Joe had never said a negative word to me in all the years I knew him. But on this day, he told me that he was about to die. I asked him to explain what was going on. He had been to the Mayo clinic in Minnesota.

They diagnosed him with a severe case of cancer of the liver. They sent him home and told him he had less than two weeks to live.

Right away, I began explaining Jesus and His healing to my friend. It took about an hour to teach him what Jesus had done. At the end, Joe, who had known absolutely nothing about Jesus, accepted Jesus as his King and received his healing by faith.

As soon as Joe and I finished, He asked me if I would do the same with his wife, Henrietta. Henrietta was also completely ignorant of the Gospel. When we finished, she too accepted Jesus.

Henrietta proclaimed that she had no doubt at all that Mr. Joe was healed. Joe took me aside and showed me a huge stack of files that the Mayo clinic had built on him. The stack included all of his medical records, their diagnosis, and their prognosis.

He told me that we were about to get confirmation of his healing. He said that they were driving to the Mayo clinic in St. Augustine Florida to be reexamined the very next day.

I didn't see Joe for another couple of months. I was very curious what had gone on with him. One day, on my way home, I saw him in his chair with a giant grin on his face. I asked Mr. Joe what had happened. He explained that they had indeed gone to the Mayo clinic in St. Augustine, and much to the doctors' shock and awe, they found no cancer in his liver.

They thoroughly examined all of the files that Joe had brought with him and could not understand how the cancer had vanished. They told him that the only explanation was a Biblical miracle.

Like the previous fellow, Joe's heart's desire was to watch his grandson grow and play with him. He was eighty years old at the time. He lived to be ninety-two. He got to see his grandson for ten more years. He died of a heart failure. Cancer never returned.

THE RUNNER

A young man, perhaps in his mid-thirties, walked into a service that I was preaching. He actually limped in, leaning on a cane. He listened intently as I taught on healing, faith, and receiving the healing that Jesus gave us on the cross. The man had suffered a severe stroke that left him paralyzed on his left side.

He had been a distance runner. He told me that he had run several marathons. He said that not running was causing him to fall into a deep state of depression.

After the service, I went to the man and explained to him how specifically and personally Jesus had healed him on the cross. My new friend bought in one hundred percent. He took his crutch and threw it behind a pew in the back of the church, and said, "I won't be needing this anymore."

The young man walked right out without the limp he came in with. I didn't see the man for a couple of months. One day, he came to see me. He looked the picture of health. I asked him how he was.

"Great! I just came by to thank you for teaching me about Jesus! I am training for the Marine Corps Marathon."

THE BISHOP

One day, a friend called me. He had just met a man that he wanted to introduce me to. The man was a wonderful preacher, beloved by all who knew him. He just happened to be black.

This most excellent man was around eighty-five when I met him. His story was astonishing. He had grown up in abject poverty. He learned at an early age to trust Jesus. He had been a very sickly child. The doctors told his mother that her frail, little son didn't have long for the world. The Bishop put his trust in Jesus. He and Jesus became best friends. He was the happiest person I have ever known or ever will know. He had what people call blind faith in Jesus.

My new pal had been raised up in a very works-based, Old Testament holiness denomination. He had no education. What he did have was a heart as big as the moon. People cherished him. He rose to the position of Bishop over several small churches. The job didn't pay much, so he made his living as a janitor. He was a janitor at the Largest Baptist Church in the area.

There was, in his community, a horrid little bar called the DOT. It was a true den of iniquity. They sold alcohol and every type of illegal drugs, especially cocaine. Prostitutes hung around the DOT, looking for and finding work.

There were frequent shootings and extreme violence every night. Folks who frequented the dump would say, "The DOT's The Spot"

Young white people from surrounding wealthy neighborhoods would go there to buy drugs. It was a booming enterprise. Going there to buy drugs, however, was a very life threatening proposition.

Wealthy young white drug addicts took the risk in order to feed their cravings. The place was a blight on the community. The Bishop hated it. He knew it made the good Christian folk in the neighborhood look bad.

He knew that many good people had been sucked into that lifestyle. He knew it was a place where Satan ruled.

The Bishop made a commitment to the Holy Spirit to do something about the DOT. He went to the elders of the huge church that he worked for. He told them that if they would give him the money, he would buy the DOT and make it into a church. They did and He did.

The Bishop did a mighty work for Jesus. The drug dealers, prostitutes, their customers, and the deadbeats that hung out at the DOT were very angry with the Bishop.

The Bishop was under the protection of the Holy Spirit. His enemy's didn't dare attack him. They knew God was on his side. I believe that when they considered attacking the Bishop, they saw two giant Angels standing beside him.

Most of the Bishops flock was dead or had moved out of the neighborhood when I met him. It was no accident that I was introduced to the Bishop. Jesus had assigned me to help him, and I knew that instantly.

I volunteered to teach a Bible Study at his church every Thursday night, to teach the Bishop the true meaning of the scriptures, and to have cars in the parking lot so that people driving by would notice that the church was alive.

I taught there for seven years. As I began to teach him about grace and faith, the Bishop got happier and happier. He called me "Teacher Man."

The Bishop told me that for the first time in his life, what he had always suspected was the truth was being revealed to him. That is why he never missed.

One night, I got a call from some of his children. They said the Bishop was dying and called me to his hospital bedside. The doctors said that he had suffered a deadly

UTI, and they told the family to come together and say their goodbyes to him.

When I arrived at the hospital waiting area, the family was gathered. There was great sadness as they waited for the Bishop to pass.

I went to see the Bishop. I asked him what he was doing in that place. The Bishop told me that he had some pain in his private place. Then he said he got sick, Mrs. Bishop called an ambulance and took him to the hospital.

The Bishop told me that he hated the place and was going home against medical advice.

A couple of days later, I got a call from the Bishop. He told me that he was at home in perfect health. And he was! Not only did he not die, he lived for eight more years. During that time, he ministered to many people.

MRS. M

A very dear friend that I have known for more than thirty years invited my wife and I to his home. His wife had been very sick and was in the middle of her second round of Chemotherapy for cancer that the Doctors told her was spreading in her body.

This wonderful woman knew nothing about Jesus except that because she believed in Him, she was saved. She was in shock, fear, sadness, gloom, and despair over the diagnosis. Her oncologist told her that even if the chemo worked, the cancer would most likely return.

Mr. M wanted to find the doctor and beat the snot out of him. He couldn't believe the doctor could say such a thing.

Mr. M steadfastly believed that his beloved wife would live and not die. The unbelief that came from the arrogant doctor was astonishing to him.

That evening, I taught Mrs. M everything you have just read about Jesus and how He has already healed her. I taught her some more power scriptures that you will learn as you continue reading.

Mrs. M attended my teaching service every week. She soaks up every word of scripture she hears. She tells everyone what happened to her. She gives our King glory with her testimony.

Mrs. M went back for an examination a week later, and the oncologist told her that the cancer was gone. Not only so, but that her body is one hundred percent clean of cancer. She knows she is healed. She has completely rejected the negative prophecy of the doctor.

There is not enough room in this book to contain all of the testimonies about Jesus and healing that I have personally witnessed.

DISCLAIMER-WARNING

Jesus taught us that the road is very narrow and few are they who find it, meaning that there are very few people who believe Him more than they do what they see or hear from the seen world.

Don't feel guilty if you are one of these. Believing Jesus takes time, practice, and education about His Word. It takes a total commitment to take off our old selves and receive newness of life. It requires a willingness and dedication to reject the notions of the past and believe Him beyond a shadow of a doubt.

NEVER GET OFF OF YOUR MEDS WITHOUT A DOCTORS PERMISSION!

Until you know in your heart that you know that you know that you believe Jesus.

If you believe that it is at all possible for illness to come into your body under any circumstances, by all means, prevail yourself of the medical science that God created.

THIS IS NOT AN ANTI-MEDICAL PROFESSIONAL, MESSAGE.

People who reject medical science when they don't totally believe Jesus are fools. I hate to hear that some works-based, unbelieving religious zealots refuse to take their children to the doctor or dentist or have them vaccinated. The results are usually disastrous.

The entire point of this chapter is that Jesus destroyed all disease on the cross. It is not possible for disease to enter our body except through unbelief. We don't have to be sick. But when we open the door to disease through doubt or our mouths, we will become ill.

Walking in health and happiness is a choice made at the deepest heart level. It is best to believe Jesus beyond a shadow of a doubt, BEFORE YOU GET SYMPTOMS!

Finally, let me show you how old scratch gets involved and has great success. Remember that Satan is the father of all liars. There is no truth in him! Satan is always running his lying mouth; that is all he is capable of doing.

The burnt up worm is on the air 24/7. If we listen to him for a nanosecond, his message sinks into our heart and mind. Then, because we choose to believe it, we speak it over ourselves, and we will have what we say.

All of the evil in the world happens for one reason: somebody listened to the lies of the great deceiver.

Pastor Dwight Keith of the Wednesday Warriors, a very large men's Bible study in Atlanta, explains it succinctly.

Dwight teaches that Satan has a flipchart. Some of you old-school people remember flipcharts. For the younger among us, he uses a white board. He operates in our mind, also known as the soul realm.

You sneeze, scratch goes to his flipchart and writes down lung cancer death. You reject lung cancer. You do not believe your sneeze is lung cancer.

The liar writes down pneumonia/death. You reject pneumonia.

Satan goes back to his whiteboard and writes influenza/death/hospitalization/sick in bed for six weeks. This is where many folks come into agreement. They seal their agreement by confessing it over themselves.

If you reject flu, he writes bronchitis on his whiteboard. Many people buy this one and say, "I have bronchitis!" Even before they go to the doctor. Guess what? If you reject bronchitis, he writes down bad cold, six weeks of coughing and hacking. Most people buy in here. Then comes the contract. The confession. Saying without a doubt, "I think I am catching a cold." Bingo!

I just recently witnessed a man catch bronchitis because he believed immediately after the first sneeze the he had been stricken with bronchitis. His confession was that he gets bronchitis every year at this time.

Even before he had any symptoms, he expected without doubt to get bronchitis based on history. So about a week later, he was suffering—and I mean suffering—from a horrible case of bronchitis.

Here is a great lie from the burnt-up cankerworm that almost everyone has fallen for. "You hugged that person or touched them, and they are contagious. Therefore, you will get what they have." You would be amazed how many people believe that lie!

I watch people at the supermarket run straight for the hand wipes to wipe down their shopping carts and their hands, and their kids' hands and arms.

They just know that if they don't do a thorough scrubbing with the hand sanitizer, they will be attacked by the Hong Kong flu, Warts, Polio, Tuberculosis, Chicken Pox, Measles, and as many diseases as their imagination will include.

Yet every single item they touch, and the money they exchange with the cashier and the bagboy are all swarming with germs.

LISTEN TO JESUS

You will learn throughout this writing that Jesus speaks to us all of the time. He told us that His sheep know His voice, and they will not obey another. He says that He knows us and calls us by our names.

If you can't hear Jesus, it is not because He is silent; it is because you aren't listening. You will know a thought is from the voice of Jesus if it is positive and brings joy and happiness. Jesus does not do or speak negatives.

When you hear a negative thought or an evil thought, you can be sure it's old blabbermouth. If the thought brings conviction of illness, judgement, condemnation, sadness, fear, anxiety, worry or any negative feelings with it, it is from the evil one.

Of course, the Holy Spirit will tell you not to walk in front of a moving train. You know the difference between instruction and negative direction.

Our prayer is that you will keep this teaching in your heart and commit to use it to walk in supernatural divine health all the days of your life.

Try this: command your brain! You are the boss of your brain. It must obey you. Command it to believe that it is impossible for an illegal invader, which is all disease, to compromise your immune system.

Command your brain to instruct all of your infinite cells to receive the healing Jesus transmitted to them on the cross. The healing is stored in their memories. They know that they have been healed. They will rise up and destroy attackers unless they are acted on by an outside force—UNBELIEF!

It may help you to remember the awful price our King paid to heal all of your maladies and diseases. Please believe that God's will is for you to walk in health, joy, and happiness. Happiness, Joy, Contentment, Health, and prosperity are all choices that we make.

Try living a healthy lifestyle. Avoid carbs and junk food. Exercise. Give up smoking and drinking alcohol. Alcohol never improved anyone's life. Alcohol is a depressant. It has a very deleterious effect on folks' predisposition to be sad and depressed.

I recently saw on Facebook a series of before and after pictures of adults who gave up chemical and alcohol addictions. The physical difference was shocking.

Jesus cannot choose for you to accept His free healing or to live a healthy lifestyle. Only you can.

CHOOSE PERFECT HEALTH!

8

Jesus Gave Us A New Life

How would you like to be able to wipe the white board of your life completely clean? You Can! Because of the loving-kindness and mercy and forgiveness of our King, you can and will have newness of life. To what extent is up to you.

We have been given the infinite Love of God! We have been given eternal salvation. We have been healed once and for all by Jesus on the cross. We have been empowered with God's own power.

We have been given the faith of Jesus Himself. We have been made free from earning by works. We have been firmly grounded in the state of Grace, not performance.

We have been given ALL things that pertain to life and Godliness. We have been given the power to speak and command. We have been given Son and Daughter status with the Creator and maintainer of all things.

When we surrender our hearts and our lives to Jesus by believing in Him, all of these things and infinitely more come to us. The sure and certain knowledge that we are entire lacking absolutely nothing, changes us. Trusting and

Believing in Jesus, and using the free gift that He gave us of His faith, changes us.

When we believe Jesus, when we buy into Him without reservation or doubt, we change. Here are some of the ways we change:

We lose the fear of lack and want. We stop speaking negative prophecies over ourselves or others. We eject negative people. We are filled with joyful visions and expectations based on believing the promises of Jesus.

NEWNESS OF LIFE COMES FROM BELIEF

When we truly and without hesitation believe Jesus, we have no need to lie, cheat, and steal to get what we want or think we need. We realize that we already have the things we fight, sometimes dirty, to get.

When we accept the love of Jesus, we no longer require the validation of others. We lose interest in thoughts of what others think of us.

When we choose to believe the Word of Jesus, we no longer require the love and acceptance of everyone.

Our affirmation comes from knowing that God Himself loves us infinitely and paid the price for our healing and forgiveness.

The validation we seek can only come from Jesus, and He valued us so much that He gave everything He had to buy us from eternal separation from Him.

Remember that song that stated "Looking For Love In All The Wrong Places?" No matter how well-meaning folk are, they cannot give us unconditional love.

People cannot give us the completely pure and unconditional love that comes without requirements and is eternal. The healing agent for all of our ills is the Love of our King and Lord, the one who created us—Jesus!

We realize that because Jesus does not judge us or others, there is no need for us to judge ourselves and others. Especially since we have been found not guilty and in perfect right standing with God because of our acceptance of the atoning, sacrificial death of Jesus.

Dr. James Richards has written a masterpiece book about newness of life titled *Moving Your Invisible Boundaries*. You will love it. If you accept Dr. Jim's guidance which originates with the Holy Spirit, you will be changed mightily. The core of the work is about taking off our old person and putting on our new regenerated self.

When we push all in on Jesus, we learn to lose the things we have no need of: fear, anxiety, worry, doubt, anger, jealousy, coveting, lust, greed, stingy-ness, cheapness, sadness, despair, meanness, smart-assed-ness, bitterness, selfishness, narcissism, racism, bigotry, hatred, division, discord, backbiting, gossip, score keeping, the need to be in control, and depression.

It is just a fact that when you truly trust in, rely on, and cling to Jesus, peace, happiness, joy, and hope replace all of the above.

The better we know Jesus and give ourselves and our issues to Him, the more we pursue Him with all that we have, the more of Him we receive.

When we know that we know that the unseen created the seen, and we strive to believe the unseen more than the seen, the better off and better connected to God we will be. God lives in the unseen.

Here is a peace-inducing promise from the Holy Spirit via Paul our teacher:

Since we consider and look not to the things that are seen but to the things that are unseen; for the things that are visible are temporal brief and fleeting, but the things that are invisible are deathless and everlasting. (2 Corinthians 4:13)

The more earthbound we are, the less God-focused and heavenly minded we are. The opposite is also true. Peace comes from focusing on the things of God. Think about this: this life is a blink of an eye. Our life in the unseen will last forever. Which seems more important?

The more we walk with God/Jesus/The Holy Spirit, the more we receive the newness of life that they paid the ultimate price to purchase for us. They want you, (fill in your name here), more than anything. They want you to be Happy and Joyful and Free!

Before we continue, please accept an editorial announcement:

When Paul talks about being baptized into Jesus, he means to become immersed in Him. He does not mean dunking, sprinkling or spraying water.

Read how the Holy Spirit dictated the explanation of this program to Paul for us:

We were buried, therefore, with Him by the baptism into death, so that just as Jesus was raised from the dead by the glorious power of the Father, so we too might habitually live and behave in NEWNESS OF LIFE.

For if we have become one with Him by sharing a death like His, We shall also be one with Him in sharing His resurrection.

We know that our old un-renewed self was nailed to the cross with Him in order that our body which is the instrument of sin might be made ineffective and inactive for evil, that we might no longer be the slaves of sin.

For when a man dies, he is freed from the power of sin among men. Now if we died with Jesus we believe that we shall also live with Him, because we know that Jesus being once raised from the dead, will never die again; death no longer has power over Him.

For by the death He died, He died to sin once for all; and the life that He lives, He is living to God. Even so consider yourselves also dead to sin and your relation to it broken, but alive to God in Jesus. (Romans 6:4–11)

By way of explanation, when Paul writes of us dying with Jesus and being baptized into death, and sharing a death like His and being dead to sin, he means that when we accept Jesus, we accept His sacrificial death.

Our pre-acceptance, pre-surrender self was dead to sin and bound for hell. When we made Jesus our Savior, we were crucified and buried with Him. Therefore, we are new and alive with and through him. We indeed have NEWNESS OF LIFE!

When Paul talks about being dead to sin and our relationship with it, he means that because we have accepted the free gift of the sacrificial death of Jesus and have therefore been forgiven of our sins—past, present, and future—our sins are no longer counted against us. We are no longer dead to sin and lost for eternity because of it.

In the next verse, Paul pleads with us not to return to a life of sin. Why? Because we so love Jesus and live in thankful contemplation of the price He paid to give us this New Life.

As a matter of fact, at the beginning of this chapter, Paul asks and answers a very important question:

WHAT SHALL we say to all this? Are we to remain in sin in order that God's grace may multiply and overflow?

Certainly Not! How can we who died to sin live in it any longer? (Romans 6:1–2)

An accurate translation of the Hebrew of that "Certainly Not" in our modern vernacular would be more like, "HELL NO!"

Paul goes on to teach us how to walk in the newness of life that we have been given:

I appeal to you therefore brothers and sisters, and beg of you in view of all the mercies of God, to make a decisive dedication of your bodies as a living sacrifice, holy and well pleasing to God, which is only your reasonable service and spiritual worship.

Do not be conformed to the patterns and behaviors of this world, this time, fashioned after and adapted to its external, superficial customs, but be transformed, changed by the entire renewal of your mind, by its new ideals and new attitudes, so that you may understand what is the good and acceptable and perfect will of God. Even the thing which is good and acceptable and perfect in His sight for you. (Romans 12:12)

When we accept Jesus, the Holy Spirit guides us and teaches us how to live a life that is good, acceptable, and perfect in His sight for us. We can no longer claim that we just do not or did not know what to do or how to behave.

After all, having learned how much God cherishes you, has done for you, and given to you, don't you want to try your best to live a life that makes Him happy? Especially since His greatest joy is your happiness?

Strip yourselves of your former nature. *Put off and discard which characterized your previous manner of life and becomes corrupt through lusts and desires that spring from delusion, And be constantly renewed in the spirit of your mind having a fresh mental and spiritual attitude.*

And put on the new nature (the regenerate self), created in God's image in true righteousness and holiness. Therefore, rejecting all falsity and being done now with it, let everyone express the truth, with his neighbor, for we are all parts of one body (Jesus's Body) and members one of another.

When angry, do not sin, do not ever let your wrath last until the sun goes down. Leave no room or foothold for the devil, give him no opportunity.

Let the thief steal no more, but rather let him be industrious, making an honest living, with his own hands that he may be able to give to those in need.

Let no foul or polluting language, nor evil word nor unwholesome or worthless talk come out of your mouth, but only such speech as is GOOD AND BENEFICIAL TO

THE SPIRITUAL PROGRESS OF OTHERS, as is fitting to the need and the occasion, THAT IT MAY BE A BLESSING AND GIVE GRACE TO THOSE WHO HEAR IT. (Ephesians 4:24)

Once made new, we want to give up wisecracks and put downs. When we are the representatives of Jesus, we lead always with love and consideration. Jesus's Peeps care and are focused on others more than themselves. Jesus's folks are always thinking how they can bless others.

A friend recently told me that you can't become a butterfly until you are willing to give up being a caterpillar. Great analogy of how we must give up our flesh in order to become a beautiful Spirit-filled person.

Here is how Paul explains newness of life in very simple terms:

I have been crucified with Jesus, in Him I have shared His crucifixion; it is no longer I who live but Jesus lives in me; and the life I now live by faith in by adherence to and reliance on and complete trust in the Son of God, Who loved me and gave Himself up for me. (Galatians 2:20)

Once we accept Jesus and make a decision to follow Him and serve Him, our goal should be to unzip our old person suit and walk away from it.

When you realize that the love of Jesus for you is personal and infinite, and you understand the price He paid for you, you will want to change. You will despise your bad actions of the past.

Do you ever get tired of your old unrepentant self? Do you get sick and tired of being angry and bitter? Are you tired of being miserable? Would you like to be a happy giving person? You can! It's a freewill choice.

IT'S UP TO YOU

When you commit to change and become a new creation in Jesus, you will want to be as much like our Master as you can be. And when you do start to change, the great payoff is how fantastic you will feel.

Self judgement and condemnation will leave you. You will sleep in peace. Fear will no longer haunt you. Anxiety, worry, and doubt will go away.

Let me make you a promise. It feels good to do good. Not boasting here, but my wife and I have dedicated our lives to helping others. The joy that we reap is immeasurable.

Now, every morning, our first thought is to ask Jesus to bring someone into our lives that day whom we can help. Every day, He does. So every day, because our focus moves from ourselves to others, we learn it feels so good to help another person. It also takes our mental focus off of us and our circumstances. I believe that focusing on giving to and helping others is the greatest psychotherapy that there is.

Here is the wrap: Jesus has given us the power and ability to become brand-new people. We have the ability to change into the person we have always wanted to be.

The key is to make a decision to believe Jesus and receive by faith what God has given us by grace. When we do, we have no need to do bad things. Happy days are ahead. Simply make a decision! Flip the switch. Reject the old you and become the new Spirit-driven you.

9

Jesus Freely Gave Us All Things

Read this pronouncement from our God-appointed and ordained teacher, Paul:

"He who did not withhold or even spare His own Son, *(Himself in the flesh)* but gave Him up for us all, will He *not also with Him freely and graciously give us all other things*?" (Romans 8:32)

Peter wrote that God has given us all things. Paul wrote that God will freely give us all things. Is there a conflict? No! What Paul meant was that at the time we accept Jesus, God will freely give us all other things. No difference at all.

Note that Paul under the direction and instruction of the Holy Spirit wrote that God will FREELY GIVE US ALL THINGS. The word *freely* means without charge. When you give a gift to a friend, you don't expect payment for that gift. You give the gift freely and joyfully. The word *graciously* means by grace. Grace is God's willingness, ability and power that has given us and done for us those things that we cannot do, or give to or for ourselves.

With this knowledge in mind, why would we plead, beg, and try to earn the things we want? Instead, what if we, as an act of faith, celebrated the fact that the desires of our heart have already been given us and praise Jesus? And thank Him for freely giving them to us? (regardless of what we see).

PAY ATTENTION, URGENT TEACHING

Yes, you believe in Jesus, but do you believe Him? That verse was given to Paul by Jesus in the person of the Holy Spirit! Please Understand! GOD HAS FREELY GIVEN US JESUS AND ALL OTHER THINGS. THIS MEANS EVERYTHING.

Here is the $64 thousand question: If God has freely given us Jesus and all other things, why have we been taught to pray and work to please God, and beg and try to get more faith, and to grovel and be good and pray in His will for things that He already freely gave us?

Yes, Folks! Whatever you want or need was given to you once by Jesus. He paid for it on the cross. He has been given everything, and you are His joint heirs.

Read this teaching from Peter, one of the original followers of Jesus. Jesus loved Peter despite his many flaws and his unbelief. Peter also loved Jesus, even though he failed to keep His commandments and instructions frequently.

SIMON PETER, a servant and apostle (special messenger) of Jesus our King, to those who have received like precious faith with ourselves in and through the righteousness of our God and savior Jesus.

WHEN YOU ACCEPT JESUS, YOU GET HIS FAITH!

There is nothing more powerful than faith. Faith is a substance that causes us to receive all of God's great and precious promises, including His Power. Without faith, it is impossible to please God.

It is a free gift. You don't earn faith. Faith is a gift that is given through the right standing or righteousness of our Lord Jesus. It is entire and complete.

Faith is received ONCE and only once. It is received by those who surrender their hearts and lives to Jesus at the time they accept Him. Jesus's faith is complete! It was earned by Him by His righteousness. Since it is a free gift, it is impossible to earn.

Accept these wishes for you from Peter:

May grace (God's willingness, ability and power that has done for us those things, that we cannot or will not do for ourselves, i.e., earn our salvation) and peace (perfect well-being, all necessary good, all spiritual prosperity, and freedom from fears and agitating passions and moral conflicts) be multiplied to you in the full personal precise, and correct knowledge of God and of Jesus our King.

Paul described this peace which was freely given to us by Jesus as a state of "undisturbed-ness." beautiful and so true. When we are disturbed, we are not being led by the Spirit, but by our flesh.

A brief teaching about faith: There are large groups of misguided, but well-meaning teachers, who believe that faith can be multiplied, added to, improved, grown, built, learned, expanded, and earned.

They base their assertion on an incorrect understanding of the Words of Jesus. They don't understand how to correctly divide the teachings of Jesus.

You see, when Jesus walked the earth, He spoke frequently to different types and groups of people. Sometimes, He was teaching you and I.

Sometimes Jesus taught the disciples. Sometimes He taught the children of Israel; He was sent to them first. Sometimes he taught gentiles (everybody but Jews), and sometimes He spoke to all of us at the same time. Sometimes Jesus taught His disciples.

The declaration you just read means that through the full and precise knowledge of Jesus, grace and peace as defined above will be yours.

The more you know Jesus, the more you ingest His Words, the more you choose to believe Jesus's Word which is Him, the more of everything you receive.

The reason is pretty simple. If you believe with every fiber in your being that Jesus has given you everything, you cannot help but have complete peace. The opposite of peace is fear and unbelief.

Why would one be anxious over something that God has already freely given them? If you thirst after peace and you want to walk in a state of grace, surrender your life to Jesus and make a choice to know and believe His words. Most folk who don't believe Jesus have never read the Gospel.

JESUS BOUGHT US EVERYTHING WE WILL EVER WANT OR NEED BY HIS DEATH ON THE CROSS.

Peter continues with a statement that is so profound as to be earth shattering. Get This:

For His divine power HAS bestowed upon us ALL THINGS that are requisite to life and Godliness through the full personal knowledge of Him Who called us by and to His own glory and excellence and virtue.

Peter, at the direction of the Holy Spirit, wrote without equivocation that God HAS (past tense) ALREADY given us ALL THINGS NECESSARY FOR LIFE and GODLINESS. He has (past tense) given us everything that we will ever need or want. Period!

Think hard now. What does that promise exclude?

How then, pray tell, would or could He give us more?

Why have we been taught that we must jump through hoops and act like circus monkeys after a stalk of bananas, to get God to give us anything? Knowing that God has already given us everything in and through Jesus, and that all we need do to receive everything is to use the free gift of Jesus's faith to gain what He gave us by grace, ask yourself how silly it is to do the following:

Beg and plead, stomp our feet, pray for the same thing over and over, get another with more faith to pray for us.

Have you ever fasted for something?

Have you ever tithed for something?

Have you ever asked someone whom you perceive has more faith than you to pray for you?

How silly is it for us to ask all of our friends and Facebook friends to pray for things for us that Jesus has already given us?

PLEASE! DO NOT BELIEVE FOR THINGS!

When you believe for something, you are permanently delaying your receipt of it. Why? Because you obviously do not believe that it has already been given to you. Doing so is an absolutely futile exercise.

As the great Bible Teacher, Believer, and Receiver, Brother Ed Everett teaches, "THE PROBLEM WITH US CHRISTIANS IS THAT WE HAVE BEEN TAUGHT THAT WE MUST BREAK INTO A ROOM IN WHICH WE ARE STANDING!"

Do you understand how confusing all of our very weird non-biblical antics are to God, Jesus, and the Holy Spirit? They know that there is not one thing that they can do for us that they have not already done.

The problem is that most people wouldn't know Jesus from a Kangaroo. Most people know nothing of Jesus, including and predominantly the pew squatters at the First Church of Gloom, Despair, and Agony.

Never heard of it? The stench in God's nostrils is the leader. They have a huge following. I have to admit that I have attended from time to time.

There was a television show during the late 1960s called *Hee Haw*. It was a country music and comedy variety show. The men of the cast performed a hilarious but oh so true tune that went like this:

Gloom, Despair, And Agony On Me!
Deep Dark Depression, Excessive Misery!
If It Weren't For Bad Luck, I'd Have No Luck At All!
Gloom, Despair, And Agony On Me!

The guys were laid out on a front porch, looking down and out, and they had a sad old saggy bloodhound lying around with them. The beautiful old hound looked like he was as depressed as they.

Don't you know several people whose world view is as above? It is perfectly logical. If you didn't know Jesus or Daddy God, and thought that it was up to you to deal with the circumstances around you, of course you would have gloom, despair, and agony.

Trying to be God is depressing and exhausting, and if you don't have God in all four persons (God, Jesus, The Holy Spirit and the Word), you are god.

Jesus gave us everything and more. Not only did Jesus give us His Faith and ALL THINGS necessary for life and Godliness, He also gave us His great and precious promises!

Peter continuing:

By means of these He has bestowed upon us His precious and exceedingly great promises, so that through them you may escape by flight from the moral decay rottenness and corruption that is in the world because of covetousness, lust and greed, and become sharers/partakers of the divine nature. (2 Peter 1:1–4)

GREAT AND PRECIOUS PROMISES

The Great And Precious Promises of which Peter writes are explained throughout this message.

They include, but are not limited to, Eternal Life, Healing, Salvation, His power, The Holy Spirit, Dominion over the evil one, Peace, Love, Prosperity, Newness of Life, A State Of Grace, and many more. Read His Word and find them. They are your inheritance in this life and in the life to come.

The Holy Spirit explained it to me like this: Pretend that you had an uncle who was a multibillionaire, and your uncle had told you that you would be his heir.

Suppose your uncle told you that you were his favorite person on the planet.

Now suppose your uncle passed away, but before he did, he told you that he gave you everything and guaranteed that promise with his will.

You would study that will night and day. You would memorize every comma. You would dig and dig until you knew that will better than yourself. Thus, you would receive all of your inheritance, and you would be deeply grateful to your uncle for treating you so graciously.

Your Daddy God did just that. He gave you exceedingly great and precious promises. Would it not be good to learn what those promises are?

STRANGELY, much of the church leadership apparently does not want us to know what our full inheritance is. Why? Well, that is covered in the chapter titled "Why You Never Heard."

The key to opening the treasure chest that God freely gave you is only to believe.

THE ROOT OF ALL LACK IS UNBELIEF

Why would we corrupt ourselves with covetousness, lust, greed, envy, and jealousy if we choose to believe that we have already been given the things that we lust for?

Why would we rob another person or place or thing to get money if we choose to believe that we have already been given all the money we can possibly spend?

Why would a person commit suicide because of a job loss if they knew for a fact that Jesus had already given them another better job? The greatest part of sin is rooted in unbelief which causes covetousness and greed. It springs from the original sin which was instigated by the snake (old slither, scratch, the evil one) convincing Eve then Adam that God was holding out on them. The father of all liars convinced them that there were things that God had not given them.

Today, we are also under the influence of that deceit. We have been taught by the church that God is a Liar. We have been taught that Jesus not only did not give us all things, but that we must earn them. The church teaches us the same thing that satan got Eve with: "Surely, He did not say."

Don't believe that statement? Go tell your Pastor, Priest, Rabbi or another spiritual leader that You can do the exact things that Jesus did and even greater things! Tell your spiritual leader that you have decided to never ask Jesus to do things for you, that He gave you the power, authority, and responsibility to do. Let me know how that works out.

The church teaches us that we are lacking things and must therefore get them. They believe and thus teach that God is holding out on us. The church has been teaching their flock to:

Beg, create prayer chains, lay hands on others, anoint folk with oil, have the elders lay hands on folk, pray repetitively, gain more faith (which is impossible), pray for them in His time and in His will and in His name, lay out a fleece, get big Ed the profound believer to pray for us, have people stand in the "gap" for us, pray and pray, and pray harder, and if that doesn't work, FAST, be baptized, and confess and repent all of our sins.

One screwy faction teaches their flock to handle deadly snakes to prove that they walk in faith. They believe that in order to receive from God, you must demonstrate this kind of faith. What they do not know will hurt them.

Jesus talked about prayer and fasting. The disciples had tried to heal an epileptic child and could not. They were trying to heal the boy with their minds and their flesh; in other words, under their own power. Nothing happened.

Jesus came and healed the boy. The disciples asked Jesus why they had not been able to heal him. Jesus replied, "BECAUSE OF YOUR LACK OF USING MY FREE GIFT OF FAITH!"

"Because of the littleness of your faith! For truly I say to you, if you have faith as a grain of mustard seed, you will

say to this mountain, Move from here to yonder place, and it will move; and nothing will be impossible for you! But this type (This degree of lack of faith) does not go out except by prayer and fasting." (Matthew 17:14–18)

Remember that the disciples didn't get Jesus's faith until after He had ascended to His Father. They had to rely on their flesh faith which varied depending on their mental state from no faith to little faith, to ever increasing faith to great faith.

The incorrect religious interpreters have made this teaching appear to mean that Jesus meant that difficult situations require prayer and fasting. So they demand that you perform both acts of work if you face a stiff challenge. WRONG! There are those who believe that their faith is not good enough to motivate God to bless them, so they "put out a fleece." I have explained in another chapter what that is all about.

There is not enough room in this book to list all of these stupid "must-do's" that men have heaped on themselves; they are legion. Every single one of them comes from the evil one. They are the antithesis of the Gospel of Jesus.

Jesus and the Holy Spirit do not require goodness from us. It's not what we do, it's what Jesus has done. The Holy Spirit speaks to us in terms such as *done* and *has been done* and *hath*.

IF ITS ABOUT EARNING SOMETHING, IT'S NOT ABOUT JESUS.

Any demand that you do something to earn something from God is based on false religion. The purveyors of performance are the false prophets of which Jesus, Peter, and Paul wrote and spoke.

The result of buying into any of these foolish behaviors is that they reinforce our unbelief, which in turn keeps us from receiving anything from God. They accomplish the exact opposite of what they are intended to do.

God's children (everyone alive) who refuse to believe the promises of Jesus lust, covet, lie, cheat, and steal to get what they refuse to believe that they already have.

They also fall into the deepest depths of discouragement, depression, resentfulness, bitterness, anger, intense competition with every other human on the planet, racism, bigotry, and most of all DOUBT, ANXIETY, WORRY, AND FEAR!

These, among other behaviors, are why Jesus declared so accurately that the path is very narrow, and few are those who find it (Matthew 7:14). In all my years in ministry, I have met very few people who actually believe everything that Jesus said.

Yes, they believe John 3:16 and Romans 10:10, the salvation scriptures. They have to accept those to avoid damnation. Yet, that is all that the vast majority of "BELIEVERS" believe.

Don't believe me? Okay, try this: give a copy of this book to your Minister or Sunday School teacher. Point out all that Jesus has done. Show them this one statement from Jesus:

If you live in me, and My Words remain in you and continue to live in your hearts, ask *WHATEVER* you wish and it *SHALL BE DONE FOR YOU!* (John 15:7)

Those who actually choose to take all of Jesus's promises literally receive everything that they desire. They receive, by faith, ALL THINGS.

Those folk have a very intimate relationship with Jesus. They are blessed beyond measure, not because of their behavior, but because they have chosen to use the faith of Jesus. They have the ability to live in a world flowing with milk and honey, and they do! If a nuclear bomb blast happened right in front of them, they would laugh and go about their business.

Most pray for things and, when they don't appear instantly, deny that they have received the answer to their prayers. Then they fall deeper into disbelief than ever. Here is our King speaking on this subject. This is a Jesus commandment:

"For this reason I am telling you, whatever you ask for in prayer, believe, trust, and be confident that it is granted to you, and you WILL get it!" (Mark 11:24)

Most people, including "Believers," only believe what they see. They rarely see that they received the answer to their prayer at the moment they accepted Jesus. So they go without, then blame Jesus. We have good reason to believe Jesus and the Gospel as it was written by the special messengers (Apostles of God).

When Peter wrote that Jesus freely gave us all things, He didn't make the story up. It was given to Him with instructions to write it by THE HOLY SPIRIT.

CREDIBILITY FROM A REAL EYEWITNESS

This is an eyewitness report (not from an unnamed source).
PAY ATTENTION.

Peter writing:

*I think it is right, as long as I am in this body to stir you up
by way of remembrance, SINCE I KNOW that the laying
aside of this body of mine will come speedily as our Lord
Jesus made clear to me.*

*Moreover, I will diligently endeavor to see to it that even
after my departure (decease) you may be able at all times
to call these things to mind. For we were not following
cleverly devised stories when we made known to you
the power and coming of our Lord Jesus, BUT WERE
EYEWITNESSES of His majesty grandeur, authority and
sovereign power.*

*For when He was invested with honor and glory from God
the Father and a voice was borne to Him by the Splendid
Majestic Glory in the bright cloud that overshadowed Him
saying, THIS IS MY SON IN WHOM I AM WELL PLEASED
AND DELIGHT, we actually heard the voice borne out
of heaven, for we were together with Him on the Holy
Mountain.*

This was such an amazing thing. Jesus only showed
Himself in His Shekinah glory twice. Once was at this event
on the Mount of Transfiguration (Matthew 17:1–6), and
when He appeared to John on the aisle of Patmos. In both
cases, the mortals who saw Him fell dead, and He had to
revive them.

This is because the human body is finite and is not tuned to the frequency of the glory of God. Our earth suits are incapable of withstanding the Glory of God.

Take a moment and read the story of the Mount of Transfiguration. It will blow your mind.

Think about it. What if Jesus showed up right now in all of His Glory and Majesty and said, "Hi there, my son or daughter, how are you today?"

You would try to dig a hole in the floor to crawl into.

And we have also a more sure word of prophecy where by you would do well that you pay strict attention, like a bright light shining in a dark place, until the day dawns and the Day Star rises in your hearts." (I highlighted this verse because of the beauty of the words.)

Yet, first you must understand this. that no prophecy of Scripture is a matter of any personal or private or special interpretation.

For no prophecy ever originated because some man willed it, but men spoke from God who were borne along by the Holy Spirit." (2 Peter 1:14–21)

Certainly you figured out that the Day Star is Jesus. Has your day dawned? Have you allowed Him to rise in your heart? You have just read the credentials of Peter's proclamation given him by the Holy Spirit that God Hath Already Given Us All Things. He was there as it happened.

King David teaches us that God has not only given us ALL THINGS ALSO, but that those things include the desires of our hearts. Read the writing of David whom God said

PASTOR ALLEN W. FLEMING

was "A Man After My Own Heart!" His words have a double meaning:

Trust, lean on, rely on, and be confident in the Lord and do good; So you shall live in the land and feed surely on His Faithfulness (Not ours. God is always faithful to His Word and His promises, He does what He says), and truly you shall be fed.

Delight yourself also in the Lord and He will give you the desires and secret petitions of your heart. (Psalm 37:3–4)

David wrote primarily to Jews who were under the law and had not received Jesus. Yet, His words are true for us as well.

Doing good is not a requirement for gaining things from God. However, when we do good, we are doubly rewarded. We get that "warm all over" feeling of knowing that we are pleasing and demonstrating our love and gratitude to our precious King.

We also receive the unrivaled feeling of helping others. Nothing feels better than to help another person.

TRY DOING THESE THINGS:

Give money to a homeless person without questioning his motives, Help a Veteran, Help a widow, volunteer to help feed the hungry, over-tip a waitress, buy a meal for a police officer, give to God. Nothing is more wonderful.

When you love God and you Love Jesus, and you love the Holy Spirit, you get the desires that are in your heart through Their free gift of Their faith.

Whatever desires you have in your heart were put there by God. When you receive Jesus, your mind and your heart do not desire evil things. Because you are submitted to Him and His will.

GOD IS NOT GOING TO GIVE US THE DESIRES OF OUR HEARTS! HE ALREADY HAS. HE CANNOT TAKE BACK WHAT HE HAS GIVEN!

Think on this, what part of ALL THINGS needs to be added to?

If you believe with every fiber in your being that Jesus has given you everything, you cannot help but have complete peace. The opposite of peace is fear and unbelief.

Let me show you a great teaching from Paul. Paul had the entire program downloaded to him during a three-year meeting with the Holy Spirit in the desert of Syria where God sent him to learn without distraction or the influence of unbelief.

Since the disciples would not teach the truth of the Gospel, God chose Paul, the worst sinner alive, to teach the Gentiles. He wanted him to be precise and correct in what he taught.

Paul knew Jesus. Jesus spoke to Him constantly. Here is a directive that Paul wrote to the church at Philippi and to us today"

REJOICE (Re-Joy yourselves. Make a decision to be full of joy and happiness and gladness.) *in the Lord always, delight, gladden yourselves in Him; again I say, Rejoice!*

Let all men know and perceive and recognize your unselfishness. The Lord is near.

DO NOT FRET OR HAVE ANY ANXIETY ABOUT ANYTHING, but in every circumstance and in everything, by prayer and definite requests, with THANKSGIVING, continue to make your requests known to God.

May I offer some clarification of that scripture? Understand that Paul was speaking to Jews who were under the law and gentiles who had yet to comprehend or hear the promises of Jesus. That is why he told them to pray with definite requests.

The keyword in that scripture is THANKSGIVING.

Why would you give thanks to God and rejoice if you didn't know that you would receive what you asked for? The knowledge that God has given us the desires of our heart is what destroys anxiety, fear, and worry.

Far too many folk today are anxious, worried, sad, depressed, and miserable because they have been taught that God is holding out on us. Paul clearly stated that the opposite is true.

My hopeful, joyful expectation is that you have read and re-read, and absorbed the message in this chapter. I want you to know joy and happiness, and to have gladness in your heart.

The Holy Spirit wants you to rest from your labors. Trying to please or get God on your side is tremendous work, pressure, and stress.

GOD HATH GIVEN YOU ALL THINGS! BELIEVE AND RECEIVE!

10

Jesus Stomped Devil Butt

This was the last chapter I wrote. The ash head hates it and me with a passion. Imagine the damage that this truth will do to the burnt-up nothing.

He has come (stupidly and unsuccessfully) against the publication of this book, stridently. He knows that no weapon formed against me or this book can or will prosper, yet he chose to fight against it hard.

One day, as I was making the final edit on this chapter, I turned on my computer to get to work. A vicious and modern malware/ransomware attack had come into my computer and locked me out.

I was hacked three years ago. From that experience, I found a fantastic company who built an impenetrable fortress around my IP and computer. It was supposed to be fail proof. The first thing I did was to call them and get them to work.

They explained that since the time I signed my contract, the malware world had increased in technology and evil intent dramatically. They explained this is how the malware got into my computer. Assuming that everything in my computer was secure, I felt safe and did not back up my computer. Huge mistake.

At that point, the evil one and his minions had this book and all of my information. It could easily be lost along with years of study, listening to the Holy Spirit and writing.

I went berserk spiritually. It is a good thing that none of my neighbors were home. I went out in my backyard and blasted the foul stench in God's nostrils for at least an hour. He had long since fled in horror.

He got his head stomped on in a way that he rarely has. I poured the acid of the Gospel of Jesus all over him, mercilessly. During my tirade, words came out of me that would embarrass the most seasoned salty drunken sailor.

The very second I walked back in the house, the diagnostics guy called me back. Strangely, miraculously he said, they were able to retrieve one hundred percent of my data. They were also able to lock the vermin out forever, and disable the data that they had stolen.

It was exactly as though nothing had ever happened. We immediately got an external hard drive and backed up the book and everything else.

After I used the power that Jesus gave me to kick the devils butt, it was as if it never happened. I just had to share that very real experience with you as a personal testimony to the power of the Word of God. Read on and you will learn how much power you have, and how little the unwanted growth has.

Satan is very real. He is alive today and wreaks havoc on whoever is ignorant of the promises of Jesus. It is impossible for demons or the evil one himself to do anything against a Jesus follower.

Those "believers" who are ignorant of his powerlessness or listen to his garbage can also be damaged. The stench in God's nostrils is still around, but he has been reduced to less than a mortal. He is not powerful, he is not smart, he is not able to do anything except lie.

And it is no wonder for, satan himself masquerades as an angel of light; so it is not surprising if his servants also masquerade as ministers of righteousness. Their end will correspond with their deeds. (2Corinthians 11:14–15)

At the very beginning of His ministry, Jesus had a spiritual battle with the evil one and stomped his butt using the best weapon we have and are charged to deploy against him: THE WORD OF GOD WHICH IS THE SWORD OF THE SPIRIT.

Here is how it went down:

THEN JESUS was led (guided) by the Holy Spirit to the wilderness to be tempted/tested by the devil.

This seems like a bizarre twist. Why would the Holy Spirit who is Jesus lead himself into the wilderness to be tempted by the burnt-up cankerworm? My thought is that it gave Him the opportunity to embarrass and defeat the evil one AGAIN in front of all of the beings in the heavenly realm.

I think that the Holy Spirit wanted to make a profound statement—that God had come to the earth in the person of Jesus to all in the heavenly realm.

And He went without food for forty days and forty nights, and later He was hungry. And the tempter (scratch) came and said to Him if you are God's Son, command these stones to be made loaves of bread.

But He replied, "It is written, Man shall not live and be upheld and sustained by bread alone but by every Word that comes forth from the mouth of God." Then the devil took Him into the holy city and placed Him on a turret, a pinnacle of the temple sanctuary.

And he said to Him, "If You are the Son of God, throw Yourself down; for it is written, He will give His angels charge over you, and they will bear You up on their hands, lest you strike your foot against a stone."

Jesus said to him, *"On the other hand, it is written also, You shall not temp/test thoroughly or try exceedingly the Lord your God."*

Again the devil took Him up on a very high mountain and showed Him all the kingdoms of the world and the glory, splendor, magnificence, preeminence, and excellence of them.

And he said to Him, "These things, all taken together, I will give You if You will prostrate Yourself before me and do homage and worship me."

Then Jesus said to him, *"Begone satan! For it has been written you shall worship the Lord your God, and Him alone shall you serve."* (Matthew 4:9–11)

Note that Jesus said, "THE LORD YOUR GOD!" Not any god or many gods or Buddha or Allah or Confucius or science; but THE LORD. Jesus made it clear that we are to worship HIM ALONE.

So if you have a coexist bumper sticker, go rip it off right now.

"Then the devil departed from Him (in one big hurry with his burnt up tail between his legs, slithering off totally humiliated)." Now the evil one knew exactly Whom He was dealing with. YIKES!

It is urgent to understand that this incident is a huge message to us. Jesus gave us the power, authority, and responsibility to do the same thing, and use the same weapon against the foul odor—THE WORD! And we will get the same result. He will run! THE WORD is like battery acid to the serpent. It scares his skin off. That is why snakes shed, regardless of what science says (just kidding).

THE DEVIL IS STILL DISGUISING HIMSELF! He and his minions, and those under his influence, are still masquerading as purveyors of truth and good. Some of satan's servants are standing in pulpits and lead Bible study groups. Their end will correspond with their deeds.

Here, Paul and the Holy Spirit are showing us one of the tricks of the burnt-up cankerworm. He disguises himself. We can't see him physically or we would laugh ourselves sick at the sight of the little ash scarred worm. We can hear him, and he is very skilled at disguising his voice.

That is how he brought sin into the world. He speaks in soft and subtle tones. Here is how a thought presented in the voice of our minds by the devil might sound:

"Hey, Mr. dump truck driver, look at that pretty girl over there!"

The driver listens and takes his eyes off of the road at the exact moment a kid on a bicycle runs out in front of Him.

"Hey, dude, all those evil rich people have got their money stored in that bank. It's full of cash. You deserve that money more than they do, and you don't like to work for the man. Go rob the joint, it will be easy."

"You are such a lovely and kind hearted person, WHY would your friend have done something so hurtful to you?"

Here is how he wins. You hear that question and go down the "WHY" road. Soon you are judging and condemning your friend. Next, you grow to be resentful of your friend. Then you act on your resentment by "payback." You will soon be bitter, then angry. You will act on your anger and do something in retribution. Satan wins.

Pretty slick, huh? The *Why* thought is subtle, but amazingly powerful in a negative and completely destructive way.

Here is a true example. A person I know sat in church all of her childhood and heard the preacher teach about how God punishes his children, and how when something bad happens, it is the result of sin.

Her deluded preacher also told her that God sometimes takes things away from us to teach us lessons. Her mother died in a horrible accident that was caused by many factors. She now hates God and will not listen to anyone talk about the love of Jesus or any other thing about Jesus.

She is just not having any of it. She has gone down the why road, but not with a friend, with God! She is judging and condemning God with no concept of the truth.

There are two opposing forces in the ether in which we travel—Negative and Positive. God is always Positive. satan is always negative.

There are three voices we hear in our minds or soul realm: our own, God/The Holy Spirit/Jesus/The Word, and the voice of the evil one.

You know your mental voice. Jesus's voice is always positive. The evil one's voice is always negative. You get to choose which voice you are led by and listen to.

THE FATHER OF ALL LIES

Here is the skinny on the stench. God created an angel, his Latin name was Lucifer or light bearer. That is the Romanized name that men created for him. He was the most beautiful, powerful, brilliant, wealthy, mesmerizing of all of God's pre-Adam creations. His body was also made of every type of music.

Every musical instrument, even those that can only be generated by nature or instruments or computers, was within him.

The angel we call Lucifer was chosen by God to be His personal guardian. Lucifer was second only in beauty, grace, and power to the triune God.

The Most powerful of all angels, Lucifer was the praise and worship leader in heaven. God created him to be perfect in every way.

Lucifer had free reign over all of the stars, galaxies, multiverses and all of infinity in space. He traveled from place to place at the speed of thought.

Lucifer was admired by all creation. Beings brought him vast financial tributes to honor him. He was the definition of charm, and He was the most beautiful of all God's creation. Lucifer's magnificence went to his head. He started suffering from delusions of grandeur.

He eventually came to believe that he would rise to the throne of God. He saw himself surpassing the greatness of God.

SO THE IDIOT STARTED A WAR WITH GOD!

He enlisted the assistance of one-third of the angels referred to in the book of Revelations as the stars. He was, as a result, hurled at the speed of light from heaven along with his accompanying angels. All were severely burned by reentry into the earth's atmosphere.

Can you imagine the pomposity, narcissism, delusion, and stupidity that came on Lucifer at the moment he concocted his rebellion? It just baffles me when I hear a teacher proclaim the wisdom of the burnt up cankerworm. Being thrown to the earth at the speed of light and being burnt to ashes as a result was just the first of many horrible defeats for the old blowhard.

Lucifer died! He is dead! There will never be another Lucifer. All that remains of Lucifer is a lowly, burn-scarred worm with a loud and persistent mouth.

The stench is not some scary looking red dude with pointy ears or a pitchfork. He is a lowly, loathsome blathering liar. As you read on, you will read how God describes him.

It is amazing to me that more people believe in the devil and his power than Jesus and His power! Do you remember the movie *The Exorcist*? A little girl spun her head around and threw up pea soup, and nobody could sleep for months after they saw it. I honestly knew people who would not open their closet or look under their beds for months after they saw that ridiculous tripe.

THE DEFEATED FOE

When Eve and Adam, believing the snake, committed the original sin of eating of the fruit of the tree of knowledge of good and evil, (there was no apple) God was heartbroken!

Why? Because until that point, Man knew nothing of evil. There was no basis for guilt or judgment. Now, because of the knowledge of evil, man could be tempted with evil and would sin habitually.

Until that point, neither man nor woman was aware of nakedness. They saw themselves as the beautiful and free creatures that they were. They needed no clothing. There was nothing to hide and no reason to hide it.

God, as He has with us, gave Adam and Eve dominion over the earth and all things in it. They, like we, were entire lacking nothing.

They had no unbelief. They didn't even know that unbelief was possible, until the slithering windbag conned them into unbelief of the Word of God. Sadly, that poison has been passed down through all of the generations of man.

It was impossible for Adam and Eve to get sick. Their belief was so strong that no disease could exist around them. Then satan introduced them to doubt.

Adam and Eve walked in the cool of the evening, holding God's hand. Wouldn't you give everything to be able to do that? You can! All you must do is make Jesus your King.

If Adam and Eve thought of something, it was theirs instantly. They traveled at the speed of thought.

Yet the hideous, slithering, filthy, disgusting liar convinced them that God was holding out on them. He pulled his number one weapon on them. He called the Word of God into question.

"Surely He did not say you would die?"

People fall for that every day and night now in this age.

Unfortunately, God's children hear that "Surely He Did Not Say" lie from many pulpits. If you have difficulty believing that, give this book to your spiritual leader and let me know their response.

The thing that crushes the heart of our precious loving Daddy is not believing Him. There is nothing more painful to God or anything that makes Him angrier.

God was explosively angry with the evil liar! He told Adam and Eve that their punishment would be ejection from perfection.

He sentenced the evil one to death and eternal damnation.

And the Lord God said to the serpent, "Because you have done this, you are cursed above all animals and above every living thing of the field; upon your belly you shall go, and you shall eat dust and what it contains all the days of your life.

"And I will put enmity between you and the woman, and between your offspring and her Offspring; He (*JESUS*) will bruise and tread your head, and you will lie in wait and bruise His heel." (Genesis 3:14–15)

The fowl stench bruised Jesus's heel by leading the sinful leaders of the Jews to have him crucified. The railroad spikes were driven through His heels, not His ankles.

One spike was driven into each heel. Understand that neither Satan nor any man could take Jesus's life. That is why the long misunderstood belief that the Jews killed Jesus is false. Our sins killed Jesus.

Jesus willingly gave up His life to ransom us from the consequences of our sins. The evil one simply inspired the Jews to call for Jesus's death and led the Romans to oblige them through his lies and deceit.

JESUS THREW SATAN FROM HEAVEN AT THE SPEED OF LIGHT

"I saw satan falling like a flash of lightning from heaven."

Pay attention!

"I have given you authority over snakes, scorpions, and every power that the evil one possesses! And NOTHING, shall in anywise harm you."

Folks, that means us! Jesus has given all of us authority and dominion over every power of the foul stench in God's nostrils and over all of his minions!

As I wrote in a previous chapter, whenever the Bible refers to snakes and scorpions, it is referring to Satan and his followers.

"Nevertheless, do not rejoice at this, that the spirits are subject to you, but rejoice that your names are enrolled in heaven." (Luke 10:18–20)

Read the Word of the Holy Spirit describing all that happened with old slither: The Holy Spirit downloaded to Ezekiel the prophet this message about satan who was hidden in the personification of the King of Babylon.

WHAT HAPPENED TO LUCIFER AND ALL WHO REBEL AGAINST GOD

God, in the person of the Holy Spirit, gave Isaiah the prophet the knowledge of what happened to satan, and about the coming of Jesus and what He would do.

God filled Isaiah with wisdom, and all should read and study his prophecies. Here is what God instructed Isaiah to write regarding satan:

The whole world is at rest and is quiet; they break forth into singing (over the destruction of the evil one). *Yes, the fir trees and the cypresses rejoice at you, even the cedars of Lebanon, saying, "Since you have been laid low, no woodcutter comes up against us. Sheol (Hades, the place of the dead) below is stirred up to meet you at your coming; it stirs up the shades of the dead to greet you — even all the chief ones of the earth; it raises from their thrones in astonishment at your humbled condition all the kings of the nations.*

"All of them will tauntingly say to you, 'Have you also become weak as we are? Have you become like (the

dead)?' *Your pomp and magnificence are brought down to Sheol (the underworld), along with the sound of your harps, the maggots (which prey on dead bodies) are spread out under you and worms cover you.*

"How have you fallen from heaven, O light-bringer and daystar, son of the morning! How you have been cut down to the ground, you who weakened and laid low the nations (O blasphemous, satanic king of Babylon!)

"And you said in your heart, 'I will ascend to heaven; I will exalt my throne above the stars of God; I will make myself like the Most High.'

"Yet you shall be brought down to Sheol (Hades), to the innermost recesses of the pit (the region of the dead).

"Those who see you will gaze at you and consider you, saying, 'Is this the man who made the earth tremble, who shook kingdoms? Who made the world like a wilderness and overthrew its cities, who would not permit his prisoners to return home?'

"All the kings of the nations, all of them lie sleeping in glorious array, each one in his own sepulcher. But you are cast away from your tomb like a loathed growth (This is why I refer to him as butt boil. I have a friend who suffers from those things. They are awful) *or premature birth or an abominable branch of the family and like the raiment of the slain; and you are clothed with the slain, those thrust through with the sword, who go down to the stones of the pit into which carcasses are thrown, like a dead body trodden underfoot."* (Isaiah 14:7–18)

If you want to get satan to shut up and leave you alone, read that proclamation from God to him. Don't be confused by the reference to the king or kings of Babylon. They were all satan in disguise. When God refers to them, He is speaking to the loathsome growth satan thought that he could hide himself in the kings of Babylon.

Babylon is the place where the ash heap landed on reentry into earth's atmosphere. Today, it is modern day Iran.

There are many wonderful Iranians who are Jesus believers. It is the spiritual leaders of Iran who are the personification of evil satan has never left that place. They obey the instruction of the Quran that demands murder for anyone who does not accept and obey it's medieval teachings.

Islam is not a peaceful, high jacked religion. All who wish to call themselves Muslim must obey the command to kill, violently destroy, and torture all infidels. Those who follow these instructions are not extremists. They are fundamental followers of Islam.

Quran Q2:191–193 says, "And kill them wherever you find them." Meaning those who will not convert to Islam. There are more than 100 commands in the Quran to attack, behead, punish with violence those who disagree with their medieval concepts.

Those who call themselves peaceful Muslims are in fact extremist, and they are not Muslim. They are considered infidels, just as anyone who rejects the teachings of the "Prophet."

Babylon was like Sodom and Gomorrah and a profane Godless city called Tyre. They were all hotbeds of idol worshippers, deviants, adulterers, promiscuous, lustful, flesh-driven, demonic sinners satan ruled them all.

satan/old scratch/ash head/butt boil/burnt up cankerworm/
The devil is nothing but a heap of ashes. He is a burnt-up
cankerworm, he and his burnt up angels (one-third of the
angels in heaven followed the evil one in the rebellion and
like him are completely without power, except that which is
given them by ignorant or deceived humans).

God revealed the same description of the evil one to the
prophet Ezekiel. This time, God identified him as the king
of Tyre. Here is what the Holy Spirit wrote through Ezekiel:
IMAGINE BEING BLASTED BY GOD LIKE THIS! WHERE
WOULD YOU GO TO HIDE?

God referred to Ezekiel as the Son of Man, meaning the
son of Adam. Here is what He instructed Ezekiel to write:

*THE WORD of the Lord came again to me saying,"Son of
man, say to the prince of Tyre* (Satan) *thus says the Lord
God:*

*'Because your heart is lifted up and you have said and
thought I am a god, I sit in the seat of the gods, in the heart
of the seas; yet you are only man (weak, feeble, made of
earth) and not God, though you imagine yourself to be
almost more than mortal with your mind as the mind of
God;*

*'Indeed, you are (imagining yourself) wiser than Daniel;
there is no secret (you think) that is hidden from you;*

*"With your own wisdom and with your own understanding,
you have gotten your riches and power and have brought
gold and silver into your treasuries;*

*'Therefore, thus,' says the Lord God, 'Because you have
imagined your mind as the mind of God (having thoughts*

225

and purposes suitable only to God Himself), Behold therefore, I am bringing strangers upon you (Jesus followers equipped with the truth of the Gospel), *the most terrible nations, and they shall draw their swords* (The Words of Jesus) *against the beauty of your wisdom, and they shall defile your splendor.*

'They shall bring you down to the pit of destruction and you shall die the many deaths of all the Tyrians that are slain in the heart of the seas. Will you say, 'I am a god' before Him who slays you? But you are only a man made of earth, and no god in the hand of him who wounds and profanes you. "You shall die the death of the uncircumcised by the hand of strangers, for I have spoken it,' says the Lord God!

Moreover, the Word of the Lord came to me saying, "Mortal man, take up a lamentation over the king of Tyre and say to him, thus says the Lord God, 'You are the full measure and pattern of exactness, full of wisdom, and perfect in beauty.

'You were in Eden, the garden of God; every precious stone was your covering, the carnelian, topaz, jasper, chrysolite, beryl, onyx, sapphire, carbuncle and emerald; and your settings and your sockets and engravings were wrought in gold. On the day that you were created they were prepared.

'You were the anointed cherub that covers with overshadowing wings, and I set you so. You were upon the holy mountain of God; you walked up and down in the midst of the stones of fire; like the paved work of gleaming sapphire stone upon which the God of Israel walked on Mount Sinai.

'You were blameless in your ways from the day you were created until iniquity and guilt were found in you.

'Through the abundance of your commerce you were filled with lawlessness and violence, and you sinned; therefore I cast you out as a profane thing from the mountain of God and the guardian cherub drove you out form the midst of the stones of fire.

'Your heart was proud and lifted up because of your beauty; you corrupted your wisdom for the sake of your splendor, I cast you to the ground; I lay you before kings, that they may gaze at you.

'You have profaned your sanctuaries by the multitude of your iniquities and the enormity of your guilt by the unrighteousness of your trade.

'Therefore I have brought forth a fire from your midst; it has consumed you, and I have reduced you to ashes upon the earth the sight of all who looked at you.

'All who know you among the people are astonished and appalled at you; you have come to a horrible end and shall never return to being.'" (Ezekiel 28:1–19)

After all that, the putrid smell was still around. Jesus, though, wasn't through with him. Here is another beating he gave the worm.

Jesus drove a nail into scumbags heart when He fulfilled the Hebrew law and freed the Jews from the bondage of works. Then He freed all others (Gentiles, Non-Jews) from the wages of sin.

Here is how our teacher Paul explains this:

And you who were dead in trespasses and in the uncircumcision of your flesh (your sensuality, your sinful carnal nature), God brought Us to life together with Jesus having freely forgiven us all our transgressions,

Having cancelled and blotted out the note (bond/Hebrew law/Ten Commandments/603 attached ordinances) which was in force and stood against us (hostile to us).

This note (with its regulations, decrees and demands) He set aside and cleared completely out of our way by nailing it to the cross.

God disarmed the principalities and powers that were ranged against us and made a bold display and public example of them, in triumphing over them in Him and in it (the cross). (Colossians 2:13–15)

HERE IS WHAT THAT SCRIPTURE MEANS:

In the days of Jesus, when the Romans defeated an army, they made an "open spectacle" of the commanding general. His soldiers were killed or imprisoned so that he had no one to command. A sign was hung around the commander's neck that read, DEFEATED FOE.

The defeated foe was dragged, bound in chains, naked through the streets of Rome. His thumbs and big toes were separated from his body so that he could never again fight. He was beaten, ridiculed, and spat upon.

His soldiers were either dispatched with extreme prejudice or imprisoned and turned into slaves or were dispersed to far distant lands. The point of this open humiliation was to demonstrate to the citizens and soldiers of Rome that the diminished man would never again be a threat.

This is precisely what Jesus did to the evil one. And Jesus did it in front of everyone in the heavenly realm.

When Jesus proclaimed that, "IT IS FINISHED!" he meant that His work was finished. He meant that during His life, He fulfilled the Hebrew laws and ordinances and nailed them to the cross.

He meant as He had proclaimed that when He was lifted up (crucified), He drew ALL MEN to himself.

I WILL DRAW ALL PEOPLE TO MYSELF.

This declaration from Jesus is so cool, and it is an unbreakable promise:

"Now my soul is troubled and distressed, and what shall I say? Father, save Me from this hour of trial and agony?

"But it was for this very purpose that I have come to this hour, that I may undergo it. Rather, I will say, Father, glorify, honor, and extol Your own name!"

Then there came a voice out of heaven saying, "I HAVE ALREADY GLORIFIED IT. AND I WILL GLORIFY IT AGAIN." Therefore the people who stood by and heard it said that it had thundered.

Others said, "An Angel has spoken to Him."

Jesus answered and said, "This voice did not come because of Me, but for your sake. Now is the judgment of this world; now the ruler of this world (satan) WILL BE CAST OUT. AND IF I AM LIFTED UP (crucified) FROM THE EARTH, I WILL DRAW ALL PEOPLES TO MYSELF." (John 12:27–32)

Jesus freed both Jew and Gentile from the sins that satan used to persecute them. satan could no longer hold their sins over those who accepted Him by calling them sinners before God. His favored weapon—extortion and blackmail—was finished.

This crushed the stench. Because of Jesus, all men were made innocent in the eyes of God, no matter what, if they gave themselves to Jesus.

ANOTHER MESSAGE FROM PAUL

"Do not be deluded or deceived, God will not be mocked or sneered at (scorned, disdained or mocked by mere pretensions of professions, of His precepts being set aside)! *He inevitably deludes himself who attempts to delude God. For whatsoever a man* sows, *that and that only is what he will reap."*

This means that when the stench mocked God, the well-known substance hit the fan. Scratch is reaping slowly and oh so painfully what He sowed.

God's mercy is limitless, and it abounds forever for those who accept, worship, and obey Him.

Not so with the devil. He is doomed. For him, there is no way out. Before he meets his end, he will suffer total and humiliating destruction and unheard of pain as the price for leading God's children away from Him.

Have you ever heard people mock the followers of Jesus as tobacco dripping, inbred, toothless idiots? It happens every day. Who might these mockers be led by?

SOME devil LIES YOU MAY HAVE HEARD:

A fish can't swallow a man.
God and the Bible are fairy tales.
You are smarter than God.
You have a higher moral compass than God.
The earth is only 6 thousand years old and God created it in six days; oh sure!
Jesus was born of a virgin and was resurrected? Right!
Jesus walked on water? I can do that if I know where the rocks are, ha ha ha.

Let's tackle some of these. If God created every single thing including quantum physics, and is in every fiber of the smallest particulate matter, holding all things together, why would it be impossible for Him to make any of these things happen?

Explain to me how a mortal human can comprehend what six days or one thousand years equal in God's world? Do any of the elitist intellectuals claim the ability to discern the difference between 1,000 years and 1,000,000,000,000 years in God's world where time does not exist?

The Bible does not say that a whale swallowed Jonah of Nineveh! It says that he was in the belly of "a large fish."

Have we identified all of the species of fish in the sea? Even if we have, why would it be impossible for the creator of all things to create a fish capable of swallowing a small man whole?

If God ever did die, everything in all the multiverses and infinite space would cease to exist. The earth and all of the stars and planets would explode.

Without God/Jesus/The Holy Spirit/The Word being the pulsating, illuminating energy that balances the opposing forces that make all things happen, nothing would exist.

One of the tricks of the great deceiver is to convince people that the Word is a made up fairytale, and that they are too smart to believe the miracles and stories contained in it. People who consider themselves dilettante logicians and super intellectuals fall into this trap very easily. Upon exhaling their last breath, the elitists know it alls will learn immediately that God is real, that hell is real, and that they made a very bad bet. On their way to hell, they will bend their knees and confess that Jesus is Lord to the Glory of God.

GOD HAS A FEW QUESTIONS FOR THOSE WHO THINK THEY ARE SMARTER THAN HE IS

"Where were you when I laid the foundation of the earth? Declare to me, if you have and know understanding."

"Who determined the measures of the earth, if you know? Or who stretched the measuring line upon it?"

"Upon what were the foundations of it fastened or who laid its cornerstone, when the morning stars sang together and all the sons of God shouted for joy?"

"Or who shut up the sea with doors when it broke forth and issued out of the womb?"

"When I made the clouds the garment of it, and thick darkness a swaddling band for it, and marked for it My appointed boundary and set bars and doors, And said, Thus far shall you come and no farther, and here shall your proud waves be stayed?"

"Have you commanded the morning since your days began and caused the dawn to know its place, so that light may get hold of the corners of the earth and shake the wickedness of night out of it?"

"It is changed like clay into which a seal is pressed; and things stand out like a many-colored garment."

"From the wicked their light is withheld, and their uplifted arm is broken."

"Have you explored the springs of the sea? Or have you walked in the recesses of the deep?"

"Have you comprehended the breadth of the earth? Tell Me, if you know it all."

"Where is the way where the light dwells? And as for darkness, where is its abode, That you may conduct it to its home, and may know the paths to its house?"

"You must know since you were born then! Or because you are so extremely old!"

"Have you entered the treasuries of the snow or have you seen the treasuries of the hail, Which I have reserved for the time of trouble, for the day of battle and war?"

"By the way, is the light distributed or the east wind spread over the earth?"

In all of their technological splendor, meteorologists cannot accurately predict the exact direction of a hurricane or where it will land. Neither can they predict the path of a tornado.

They cannot, with any accuracy, predict when snow will fall or in what amounts and where. They will never know how the wind originates or where it is going, even with the use of their multimillion dollar equipment.

"Who has prepared a channel for the torrents of rain or a path for the thunderbolt, To cause it to rain on the uninhabited land and on the desert where no man lives, To satisfy the waste and desolate ground and to cause the tender grass to spring forth?"

"Has the rain a father? Or who has begotten the drops of dew?"

"Out of whose womb came the ice? And the hoary frost of heaven, who has given it birth?"

"The waters are congealed like stone, and the face of the deep is frozen

"Can you bind the chains of the closest of stars called Pleiades or lose the cords of the constellation Orion?"

"Can you lead forth the signs of the zodiac in their season? Or can you guide the stars of the Bear with her young?"

"Do you know the ordinances of the heavens? Can you establish their rule upon the earth?"

"Can you lift up your voice to the clouds, so that an abundance of waters may cover you?"

"Can you send lightning's, *that they may go and say to you, Here we are?"*

"Who has put wisdom in the inward parts? Or who has given understanding to the mind?"

"Who can number the clouds by wisdom?"

"Or who can pour out the water bottles of the heavens when heat has caused the dust to run into a mass and the clods to cleave fast together?"

"Can you hunt the prey for the lion? Or satisfy the appetite of the young lions when they couch in their dens or lie in wait in their hiding place?"

"Who provides for the raven its prey when its young ones cry to God and wander about for lack of food?"(Job 38:4–30)

This direct line of questioning continues for another thirty verses. I urge you to read them and present them to anyone in your network who thinks that God is a fairytale. There are seventy-seven of them. So you think the SAT was hard? Let me know how you do.

Consider, if you will, asking just one of these questions to those who aspire to out-think the creator: *"Have you explored the springs of the sea?"*

If so, please write and let me know how deep the Mariana's Trench in the Pacific Ocean is. Up until very recently, scientists did not even know that there were springs in the sea. Here is another question for the super educated intellectual: *"Have you comprehended the breadth of the earth?"*

Try this one on an elitist snot-nosed atheist professor! *"Where is the way where light dwells?"*

Let's simplify God's question so that the Godless Physicist can understand it. Where, oh genius, does light begin and end?

The next time a person gives you that look when you tell them that God created everything, give them these two chapters as a homework assignment. People think that those who accept every Word of the Bible are Neanderthals. They claim that Christians don't believe in evolution! HUGE LIE!

If we didn't believe in evolution, we WOULD be idiots. That everything is constantly evolving is clearly obvious.

What followers of the Way do not believe is Darwinian evolution. If you believe Darwin, it is not we who are stupid, it is you. Darwin's description of evolution is a genuine fairytale. It is, in fact, a ridiculous theory. Darwinists are the highest form of Anti-Intellectualists. The buffoonish Darwinists sneer at intelligent creation.

There is NO fossil or other scientific evidence of cross-species mutation or of the creation of new life, PERIOD; and as it is utter nonsense and completely impossible there will never be any.

Tell me this, Darwinist, if man evolved from primordial ooze, who created the primordial ooze? I will make a deal with any Darwinist. If you can show irrefutable evidence of one cross-species mutation from primates to homo sapiens, I will eat this book right in front of you and give you an hour to draw a crowd.

The Bible is a fairytale? There is more evidence that Jesus existed than there is evidence that John Kennedy existed.

Science and the Bible never disagree. It is not possible for science to refute the Bible, because God created science.

PETER'S LESSON ON THE EVIL ONE

Pay attention to the warning that Peter gave us about the Liar:

Therefore, humble your selves, demote yourselves in your own estimation; under the mighty hand of God, that in due time He may exalt you.

Casting the whole of your care; all of your anxieties, all your worries, all your concerns, once and for all on Him, for He cares for you affectionately and cares about you watchfully. Be well balanced; temperate, sober of mind, be vigilant and cautious at all times for that enemy of yours, the devil, roams around like a lion roaring in fierce hunger, seeking someone to seize upon and devour.

Withstand him; be firm in faith against his onset — rooted, established, strong, immovable and determined, knowing that the same sufferings (fighting to live in the spirit and not the flesh is what is meant by suffering) *are appointed to your brotherhood* (the whole body of Jesus Believers throughout the world), *and after you have suffered* (meaning fought, stood strong) *for a little while, the God of all grace Who has called you to His own eternal glory in Jesus will Himself complete and make you what you ought to be, establish and ground you securely, and strengthen and settle you.* (1 Peter 5:6–10)

I love those Words from the Holy Spirit given to Peter as a description of our loving Daddy. Never forget them: "THE GOD OF ALL GRACE."

Know that the devil only has one weapon! His deceit and your acceptance of his thoughts and lies. Even though the unwanted growth is powerless but to lie, he has an arsenal of lies that are nearly perfectly constructed. He uses them perpetually and has a tremendous closing ratio.

Jesus has specifically identified these areas in which scratch operates with great success:

1. The cares and anxieties of this world,
(a.) the fear of what other people think of me.

2. The pleasure and delight and false glamour and deceitfulness of riches,

3. Craving and passionate desire for other things, creep in and suffocate the Word, and it becomes fruitless."

(Mark 4:19)

THE FEAR OF WHAT OTHERS THINK

I actually know people who are dying, rather than speak or even choose to believe the Gospel of Jesus, in fear of what others will think. It actually happened to a man I ministered to. The man was eaten up with cancer. I was asked to come and pray with him. The man had no chance except to hear and make a decision to believe the truth—that Jesus destroyed cancer on the cross.

I chose not to be namby-pamby with this fellow. I spent an hour explaining the Gospel of Jesus to Him. It has been said that I didn't give the man a chance to get a word in edgewise, which is true. There wasn't time for debate.

The man told His son, who is a non-believer, what the Holy Spirit had told Him through me, which was only pure scripture. The son and the man's wife called BS on Jesus. That was all she wrote.

The man was so concerned about what his family thought and his traditional religious views that he would rather die than believe or even investigate the scriptures I taught him. Very sad.

There are many people headed straight to hell, because they are so afraid of the opinions of the cool people that they could never accept the truth of the Gospel. These folk, and sadly there are many of them, are more concerned about their success in this "wisp of smoke" life than where they will spend all of eternity.

BE VERY CAREFUL WHAT YOU HEAR!

Paul was under assault by a messenger from satan that followed him everywhere he went. Paul asked God to remove the thorn from his flesh three times. Jesus's response is the perfect teaching on how to defeat butt boil.

And to keep me from being puffed up and too much elated by the exceeding greatness (prominence) of these revelations, there was given me (by the evil one) a thorn (a splinter) in the flesh, a messenger of Satan, to rack and buffet and harass me, to keep me from being excessively exalted.

Three times I called upon the Lord and besought Him about this and begged that it might depart from me; But He said to me:

"My Grace Is Enough For You (sufficient against any danger and enables you to bear the trouble manfully); For My Strength And Power Are Made Perfect And Show Themselves Most Effective In Your Weakness." (2Corinthians12:7–9)

There it is! We have been given dominion over the evil one and all of his powers and demons and servants. No weapon forged against us can prosper. Nothing shall in anywise harm us. Jesus's Grace is sufficient in every situation in our lives!

JESUS STOMPED THE devil's BUTT AND GAVE US THE POWER, AUTHORITY, AND RESPONSIBILITY TO STAND ON his HEAD AND TWIST.

Read this declaration from Jesus to Peter:

"Simon, Simon, listen, satan has asked excessively that all of you be given up to him out of the power and keeping of God, that he might sift all of you like grain, But I have prayed for you Peter *that your faith may not fail:* and when you yourself have turned again, strengthen and establish your brothers." (Luke 22:31–32)

The point being that it is not Jesus's responsibility to fight scratch for us! Our faith, which is actually Jesus's faith that we received at the time we accepted Jesus, will destroy the evil one. It's up to us to use it.

Here is a short but powerful teaching from the disciple James:

So *be subject to God. RESIST THE DEVIL AND HE WILL FLEE FROM YOU.* (James 4:7)

Paul taught us EXACTLY how to fight the evil one and those who come under his influence. Follow this instruction and you will never have a problem with old ash face:

In conclusion, BE STRONG IN THE LORD (be empowered through your union with Him]; draw your strength from Him [that strength which His boundless might provide).

Put on God's WHOLE ARMOR (the armor of a heavy armed soldier which God supplies), that you may be able to successfully STAND UP against all the strategies and the deceits of the devil.

For we are not wrestling with flesh and blood (contending only with physical opponents), but against the despotisms, against the powers, against the master spirits who are the world rulers of this present darkness, against the spirit forces of wickedness in the heavenly supernatural sphere.

Therefore put on God's complete armor, that you may be able to resist and stand your ground on the evil day of danger, and having done all the crisis demands, to stand firmly in your place.

Stand therefore hold your ground, having tightened the belt of truth around your loins and having put on the breastplate of integrity and of moral rectitude and right standing with God. And having shod your feet in preparation to face the enemy with the firm footed stability, the promptness, and the readiness produced by the good news of the Gospel of Jesus.

Lift up over all the SHEILD OF FAITH. UPON WHICH YOU CAN QUENCH ALL OF THE FLAMING MISSILES OF THE WICKED ONE. And take the HELMET OF SALVATION (which you get upon accepting Jesus.) *and THE SWORD*

THAT THE SPIRIT WIELDS, WHICH IS THE WORD OF GOD.

These are the weapons given us by the blood of Jesus to use against the slithering liar and his crew:

THE BELT OF TRUTH—The Word Of God. The Gospel of Jesus.

THE BREASTPLATE OF RIGHTEOUSNESS/ INTEGRITY—The right standing we have with God because of the blood of Jesus. Our "sinless-ness" in the eyes of God.

BATTLE BOOTS—to wear on our spiritual feet, to stomp the worm, which is the stability given us by the Gospel.

THE SHEILD OF FAITH—The free gift of Jesus's faith against which not even a nuclear tipped missile can prosper.

THE SWORD OF THE SPIRIT—The Gospel of Jesus! If you want to see old soot haul butt, start quoting the Gospel.

The Shield of Faith is a defensive weapon. The Sword of The Spirit, which is the Gospel of Jesus, is an offensive weapon. We are to use it to attack the evil one and his minions. We are not to sit by passively and wait for the butt boil to make the first move.

We have been given every weapon we will ever need. It is up to us, however, to use them.

Remember the statement of Peter that you just read? Peter wrote that butt boil goes about AS a roaring lion seeking whom he may devour. That can't be you if you are surrendered to Jesus and accept the power that He gave you.

Do you remember the cowardly lion in *The Wizard of Oz*? That is a great picture of the stench, except for the fact that he is only as large as a burnt-up worm. Old male lions don't hunt, they roar. The vicious lionesses hunt. The lionesses set a trap for their victims. The pride waits in joyous expectation of their victims. They send the old lion in the opposite direction of their killing zone. The lion roars as loud as he can. The victims run in the opposite direction of the roar, right into the pride. BOOM! OUCH!

Old scratch does the exact same thing. He can't destroy anything. So he sells his BS to his victims, they listen, and commit behaviors that destroy them.

NEVER FEAR THE DEVIL!

STOMP ON HIM!

11

Why You Have Never Heard

If I were you, I would be asking myself why I have never heard the life-changing, empowering scriptures this book is based on, taught anywhere until now.

LET ME MAKE THIS CLEAR: THE VAST MAJORITY OF PASTORS ARE GOOD PEOPLE WITH NOBLE INTENTIONS. I AM NOT ATTACKING YOUR PREACHER!

I asked God why so little of His Gospel is taught from the Pulpit or in the media. I asked the Holy Spirit to show me why the Great and Precious Promises of Jesus are fought so hard by the mainstream church.

This is how The Holy Spirit answered my question: Shame (being embarrassed to believe or teach the controversial promises of Jesus), Deceit, Ignorance, Tradition, Unbelief, Greed, and The Cares Of This World/ The Fear Of What Other People Think.

In this chapter we will examine each of these.

PLEASE REJECT THE SPIRIT OF OFFENSE

Often, when we hear or read a teaching that disputes
our current theology, the evil one comes with the spirit of
offense. I promise you that some of you dear readers will
find some of this teaching to be accusatory and an attack
on age old doctrine and ritual.

Some of you will be angry about what you are about
to read. Please relax and check the scriptures. Please
examine the scriptures to learn if what I wrote is truth.

In Alcoholics Anonymous they have a famous phrase
to describe our natural offense and defense when we
are presented with facts that contradict our paradigms:
"Condemnation prior to Investigation."

Buckle your seat belts, we are in for a bumpy ride. Know
that I am merely marching to the orders given me by the
Holy Spirit.

*Please read my marching orders from the Author, The Holy
Spirit. You may remember them from the Foreword, but they
need repeating here:*

*I CHARGE YOU in the presence of God and Jesus, who is
to judge the living and the dead, and by His coming and
His Kingdom:*

*Herald and preach the Word! Keep your sense of
urgency, whether the opportunity seems to be favorable
or unfavorable. Whether it is convenient or inconvenient,
whether it is welcome or unwelcome, you as preachers of
the Word are to show people in what way their lives are
wrong.*

And convince them, rebuking and correcting, warning and urging, and encouraging them, being unfailing and inexhaustible in patience and teaching.

For the time is coming when people will no longer tolerate or endure sound and wholesome instruction, but having ears itching for something pleasing and gratifying, they will gather to themselves one teacher after another to a considerable number, chosen to satisfy their own liking and to foster the errors they hold, and will turn aside from hearing the truth and wander into myths and manmade fictions.

Paul was describing the watered-down or totally false "gospel" message of today, especially those who are perpetuating this new "liberal Christianity." Any diversion from the Words of Jesus is vile to God. Universalists gag God!

"As for you, be calm and cool and steady, accept and suffer unflinchingly every hardship. Do the work of an evangelist. Fully perform all the duties of your ministry!"

DECEIT

The goal of satan is not to send people to hell. It is to steal the power of Jesus from His children. He has been amazingly successful. Very few, if any "believers," know the promises of Jesus. Fewer still believe them.

Among the people in your circle, how many know that they have been given Jesus's power and the responsibility to use it? How many friends of yours know that they have been healed and cannot get more healed than they are? How many of your peeps know that healing is gained by believing and speaking, not praying? Do you know many people who know that Jesus has already given them ALL THINGS that pertain to life and Godliness? Do you know many who understand that when Jesus said, "*IT IS FINISHED,* He meant it and that He cannot change anything that came out of His mouth?

How many folk do you know who understand that the reason Jesus gave us His faith, His power, and His great and precious promises was so that we would use them to produce "much fruit?"

Satan wants to see disease, poverty, misery, lack, want, lust, covetousness, anger, bitterness, competition, racism, bigotry, resentment, un-forgiveness, meanness, but most of all unbelief spread to all "Believers" so their testimony is fouled.

One touchdown for the evil one is for men to teach His children that God is holding out on them, and needs to be talked into meeting their needs.

The devil wants to see the Gospel of Jesus minimized, obfuscated, denied, ignored, scoffed at, mocked, scorned, miss taught, not taught, hidden and derided, and most of all UNBELIEVED.

The scum of the earth succeeds when God's children are ignorant of His promises and live as a result in powerless, ill, hopeless, joyless, purposeless lives through his deceit.

Scratch loves it when God's children are taught a false or minimalist gospel of tradition and works, or legalism and impossible to achieve performance demands.

If you really want to make the devil happy, put a coexist bumper sticker on your car. Tell others that there are other ways to heaven than through the salvation of Jesus. If you want to make the one who comes to kill, steal, and destroy giddy, tell folk that they must obey the commandments of Moses.

I describe what the burnt-up cankerworm has accomplished among "believers" as "THE GREAT DECEPTION."

GOOD NEWS OF GREAT JOY

Remember reading this promise from Jesus?

"Come to me all of you who are tired and weary and are heavily loaded and overburdened, and I will give you REST (I will ease and relieve and refresh your souls). Take My yoke upon you and learn of me, for; I am gentle and humble in heart, and you will find rest (relief and ease and refreshment and recreation and blessed quiet) *for your souls. For My yoke is wholesome* (useful, good—not harsh, hard, sharp or pressing, but comfortable, gracious, and pleasant), *and My burden is light and easy to be borne."*

If that is not the Gospel you have been hearing, it is not the Gospel of Jesus. Run, don't walk away. Is trying to beg God and sell Him on your worthiness in order to gain something from Him a light yoke? Is trying to please God by your works and behavior a light yoke? Is keeping the Ten Commandments and the attached 603 ordinances a light and easy to bear burden?

Remember this message from God to us through Gabriel God's personal Angel and through the Heavenly Host, delivering the precise words of God when He came into His earth suit?

Gabriel appeared to a group of shepherds guarding their flocks at night. And the glory of the Lord flashed and shone all about them, And they were terribly frightened.

But the Angel said to them, "Do not be afraid, *(Uh-oh, too late, already soiled my britches)* for behold *(pay attention),* I bring you *GREAT NEWS OF GREAT JOY WHICH WILL COME TO ALL PEOPLE."*

I know you read this in a previous chapter, but it is urgent to understand. Please do not forget this! If what you are hearing from the pulpit or any other source is not GREAT NEWS OF A GREAT JOY WHICH SHALL BE TO ALL OF PEOPLE, IT IS NOT THE GOSPEL OF JESUS!

Pay strict attention here! ALL PEOPLE MEANS ALL PEOPLE! Not just the holier than thou front row pew sitters at the first church of the frozen chosen!

"All people" includes sinners and scumbags and less than perfect in the flesh people. Yes, Ned the wino! Yes, Matilda the prostitute. Yes, Jose the abortion doctor! Yes, Alonzo the drug addict! Yes, Granny the backbiting gossiper! Yes, people with nose rings and tat's. Yes, LGBT people. God has saved them all!

The greatest news that Jesus hears is when one turns away from a life of sin and/or a life of trying to please Him by behavior or a life of following a false religion or no religion, and comes back to Him with love in their hearts.

Study this message from Jesus!

What man of you, if he has a hundred sheep and should lose one of them, does not leave the ninety-nine in the wilderness and go after the one that is lost until he finds it?

And when he has found it, he lays it on his own shoulders, rejoicing. And when he gets home, he summons together his friends and neighbors, saying to them, "Rejoice with me, because I have found my sheep which was lost."

Thus, I tell you, there will be more joy in heaven over one especially wicked person who changes his mind, abhorring his errors and misdeeds, and determines to enter upon a better course of life, than over ninety-nine righteous persons who have no need of repentance.

Or what woman, having ten silver drachmas each one equal to a day's wages, if she loses one coin, does not light a lamp and sweep the house and look carefully and diligently until she finds it?

And when she has found it, she summons her women friends and neighbors, saying, "Rejoice with me, for I have found the silver coin which I had lost."

Even so, I tell you, there is joy among and in the presence of the angels of God over one especially wicked person who repents, changes his mind for the better, heartily amending his ways, with abhorrence of his past sins.

How much more clearly could Jesus explain to us how much He celebrates the return to the fold of even one lost sheep?

Does what you have read about God and Jesus demonstrate their capacity to HATE any of their creation? Yet, I hear the message from some believers that "God Hates Adulterers, God Hates Gay People, God Hates Divorce And The People Who Get Divorced."

Does anything you have read indicate that any group of people are greater or less than another in God's eyes? In some denominations, people who get divorced and remarry must abstain from sex in order to take communion. In some denominations only those who are sinless or have been baptized are allowed to participate in communion. I know one mother whose daughter sought to be baptized in the tradition of her denomination. The mother told her daughter she could not receive communion until she was baptized.

What do you think that teenage girl did? Of course, she said, "Screw this! I don't want any part of your mean-ass God!"

Communion isn't drinking grape juice and eating that weird piece of paper. It means to eat the Word of Jesus, which is His flesh. It means to make a conscious decision to make His Words the energy source of your life. Taking communion is to drink His blood, which means to make a decision to believe that Jesus guaranteed every Word He pronounced with His own blood (John 6:53).

Communion is meaningless in the way that we have chosen to do it. What does it gain a person to make an open show of nothing? Who do you know who understands what taking communion means?

Communion is not a public display! It is a private commitment between you and Jesus, one that will absolutely change your life forever. There is no prerequisite for communion! Woe on those who teach this nonsense!

DO NOT BE DECEIVED! LEARN OF JESUS! THE REAL JESUS! THE ONE WHOSE BURDEN IS EASY AND WHOSE YOKE IS LIGHT!

SHAME

Paul, our anointed and Jesus appointed teacher, Knowing how "edgy, dangerous, controversial, and even life-threatening" the Gospel of Jesus is, wrote this:

For I am not ashamed of the Gospel (good news) *of Jesus, for it is God's power working unto salvation* (for deliverance from eternal death) *to everyone who believes with a personal trust and a confident surrender and firm reliance, to the Jew first and also to the Gentiles.* The Words of Jesus are the engine that feeds, gives life, brings health, power, all things necessary for life and Godliness and salvation to those who steadfastly believe each one of them. (Romans 1:16–17)

THE WORDS OF JESUS ARE SPIRIT AND LIFE!

Jesus made the following declaration to the Jews who insisted on trying to please God by their behavior and to those doing and teaching the same today.

"It is *the Spirit Who gives life* (He is the Life giver); *the flesh conveys no benefit whatever* (there is no profit in it). My Words are Spirit and Life. *(John 6:63)*

This is why accurate and complete knowledge of every Word of Jesus is so important! His Words Are Life!

WARNING FROM THE KING OF KINGS:

"Therefore, everyone who acknowledges Me before men and confesses Me, out of a state of oneness with Me, I will also acknowledge him before My Father Who is in heaven and confess that I am living in him.

"But whoever denies and disowns Me before men, I also will deny and disown before My Father Who is in heaven." (Matthew 10:32–33)

BEING ASHAMED OF THE GOSPEL, JESUS'S WORDS, IS THE EXACT SAME THING AS BEING ASHAMED OF HIM!

"And the WORD, (Jesus, God Himself) became flesh (human, carnate) and tabernacled (fixed His tent of flesh, lived awhile) among us; and we actually saw His glory (His honor, His Majesty), such Glory as an only begotten Son receives from His Father, FULL OF GRACE AND TRUTH! (John 1:14)

TRADITION

And the Pharisees and scribes kept asking Jesus, "Why do Your disciples not order their way of living according to the traditions handed down by the forefathers to be observed, but eat with hands unwashed and ceremonially not purified?"

But He said to them, "Excellently and truly so that there will be no room for blame, did Isaiah prophesy of you, the pretenders and hypocrites, as it stands written: These people constantly honor me with their lips, but their hearts hold off and are distant from me."

"In vain, fruitlessly and without profit do they worship ME, ordering and teaching to be obeyed, as doctrines the commandments and precepts of men.

"You disregard and give up and ask to depart from you the commandment of God and cling to the tradition of men, Keeping it faithfully and carefully.

"You have a fine way of rejecting thus thwarting and nullifying and doing away with the commandment of God in order to keep your tradition (your own human regulations!" (Mark 7:5–9)

Our King was referring to the oral tradition of the Jews. They believed that the 603 ordinances were law. Jesus told them bluntly that they were manmade traditions and not law. He was angry that the Jews honored those traditions above their relationship with God and His teachings. Just as many do today.

If you are in judgment of the Jews, consider the traditions that "Believers" worship:

Going to church on Sunday because it is the sabbath day. Actually the Sabbath has nothing to do with "Christians." It is a day that God demanded be set aside for the children of Israel to remember their captivity and deliverance from Egypt.

I grew up in a predominantly Jewish community in Tampa Florida. As I recall from going to Synagogue with my friends, the Shabbat begins a few minutes before sundown of Friday evening and lasts until three specific stars are seen on Saturday night. Not Sunday.

There is no requirement for "Christians" to observe the sabbath. In fact, Jesus declared that He is the King of the Sabbath. That being so, if Sunday is the Sabbath day, what is Monday?

There are so many traditions in the church of Jesus that we don't have enough pages to write them on. Surely, you can think of many more traditions that the religious among us consider more important than the Gospel.

Tradition is very poisonous. Sticking with incorrect theology and doctrine, because your denomination and your family always has, happens every day.

Most of you are too young to have ever heard this old hymn, but it says it all about tradition:

Gimme that old time religion,
Gimme that old time religion,
Gimme that old time religion it's good enough for me.
It was good enough for Grandpa,
It was good enough for Grandpa,
It was good enough for Grandpa
It's good enough for me!
Gimme that old time religion,
Gimme that old time religion,
Gimme that old time religion,
It's good enough for me.
It was good enough for the Jewish children,
It was good enough for the Jewish children,
It was good enough for the Jewish children,
It's good enough for me!

HOW DO YOU BREAK TRADITION?
WHO HAS THE COURAGE TO GO FIRST?

Think how difficult it would be for an honest clergyman to break from tradition.

Think about this: how do you explain to an entire denomination that you believe that Jesus has given anyone who steadfastly believes in Him His power, when no-one— and I mean no-one in your denomination—has ever repeated those words?

How do you stand in the pulpit and tell your flock that the Holy Spirit has declared that because of the sacrifice of Jesus, there is no one living or dead that can qualify to be the mediator between men and God, especially when your entire denomination is built around the opposite?

How do you tell your flock that for 2,000 years they have been doing it wrong? How do you tell your charges that they are not to worship or pray to anyone except the Holy Spirit, Jesus or God when they have been taught differently by your entire denomination?

How do you stand in the pulpit and tell your congregation that the requirement to be baptized and repent of every sin they have ever committed, and to confess every sin that they have ever committed, is non-biblical hooey when your denomination has been putting that yoke on Jesus's children for thousands of years?

How could you possibly explain to your congregation why you have never taught them the truth of the Gospel, if you ever dared to begin teaching it?

How could you explain why you have never taught your congregation or denomination that Jesus has already given us everything that you have been teaching them to fervently beg Him for?

How can you suddenly teach your flock that Jesus destroyed all illness by dying from every disease known and unknown to man on the cross when you have been teaching them to beg for healing for themselves, and others, for your entire career?

What Preacher can admit that he has led his flock in the wrong direction by teaching them to pray for things that Jesus has already given them?

What Father would suddenly admit to his family that he has led them in believing entirely wrong theology, and that it is time to change and believe the complete Gospel?

Men have told me that they have read my teachings and know the truth, but would NEVER tell their wives what they have learned for fear of what they might say, think or do.

There are people who support my ministry, Throne of Grace Ministries, Inc., who hide their giving from their friends, spouses, and relatives for fear of what they might think.

Only two of my relatives have shared my books or teachings with others. I have friends who would never hook me up with their inner circle because of fear of what they would think.

Many people refer to me as "my friend Allen," not Pastor Allen, because they are embarrassed by what I teach.

What would happen to a Preacher who told his flock that they were going to change the way they pray from begging to thanking and praising Jesus for giving them all that they will ever need or want once?

What Preacher would have the guts to admit that our relationship with God is entirely based on Grace through Faith, when he has been teaching them works as long as he has been in the pulpit? What Priest or Preacher would have the wherewithal to admit publicly that Jesus NEVER commanded men to confess their sins, one to another or even to Him?

Can you imagine a preacher suddenly teaching a flock of "believers" that they have supernatural powers, Jesus's power, when he has been teaching them to grovel before God, and trying to manipulate Him into doing what they want?

Would any Priest tell His flock that the Pope is just a man and one who is flawed like all of us, and one who knows little of the Gospel? No offense to my Catholic friends. This is not a shot at you.

How much damage would it do to organized religion if these scriptures got taught from the pulpit?

Paul:

"FOR THERE IS ONLY ONE GOD. AND ONLY ONE MEDIATOR BETWEEN GOD AND MEN. THE MAN JESUS!" (1 Timothy 2:5)

Jesus:

"AND DO NOT CALL ANYONE ON EARTH (In the church) FATHER. FOR YOU HAVE ONE FATHER, WHO IS IN HEAVEN" (Matthew 23:9)

OFFENSE, WARNING, WARNING, WARNING

This next teaching from Jesus is highly offensive to some.

If it melts your minds or hurts your theological paradigms to the point that you just can't take it, just forget that you read it.

Jesus was still speaking to the people when behold, His mother and brothers stood outside, seeking to speak to

Him. Someone said to Him, "Listen, Your mother and Your brothers are standing outside, seeking to speak to you."

But He replied to the man who told Him, "WHO IS MY MOTHER, AND WHO ARE MY BROTHERS?"

And stretching out His hand toward, not just the disciples but all in attendance, He said, "HERE ARE MY MOTHER AND MY BROTHERS. FOR WHOSOEVER DOES THE WILL OF MY FATHER IN HEAVEN IS MY BROTHER AND SISTER AND MOTHER." (Matthew 12:46–50)

Those three scriptures knock down the power of Pastors, Ministers and Priests, The Pope, and worshipping and praying to the Virgin Mary. They destroy the whole Priestly confession deal. What would happen to the Catholic church if they got out? I love Catholics!

My Partner is a Catholic, and I promise you He has a deeper knowledge of the Word and a more personal relationship with Jesus than most seminarians I have met.

I am not attacking the Catholic Church or its traditions or its members. That is not my assignment. I am merely reporting the scriptures.

Protestants operate in their goofy manmade traditions as well. This crazy dependence on Jewish Tradition in the Protestant church is 180-degrees opposite to the teaching of Jesus, but it is tradition. I mean teaching the Ten Commandments to those who are not and never have been Jewish.

Certainly you have seen protestant churches with the Ten Commandments posted on signs outside of their church.

Do you remember Christians fighting to have the Ten Commandments taught in school?

Protestants insist on this baptism by water ritual. You read in another chapter about how that tradition came to be, and how it is a Hebrew regulation that has nothing to do with "Believers."

Protestants have the nonsensical tradition of open communion that you just read about.

IGNORANCE

Ignorance is one reason for not teaching the correct Gospel. I believe that ignorance of the Gospel and the complete teachings of Jesus is like a cloud that hangs over seminaries and training grounds for denominational ministers. I believe that ignorance of the teachings of Jesus is systemic.

Jesus said of us that we will know His followers by their fruit. If the true Gospel was being taught in seminaries or colleges, the flocks of the graduates would be doing the same works that Jesus did and even greater works than those.

They would be happy and joyous and full of love. They would be speaking good things into existence instead of begging God for what He has already given.

If the seminaries were teaching the complete Word of Jesus, the graduates would have an aura of love, joy, and peace. Sick people would come to them and without any kind of ritual. They would be healed by standing in their presence. If the seminarians actually believed that they had Jesus's power and even greater, and the responsibility and authority to use it, their miraculous works would be front page, lead story news all day, every day. There would be no time to report on politics or world news.

Mentally ill folk, especially severely depressed people, would listen to them and throw away their drugs, because they would be so full of love and peace and joy that they would never be depressed again.

Have you ever attended a church service and left feeling worse than you did when you went? It happens every Sunday, and it is the complete opposite of Jesus's love.

If Jesus's children actually knew His message and promises, we would have a Jesus day every year like the Fourth of July or Cinco de Mayo or the feast of the Epiphany.

There would be fireworks, music, laughing, and dancing every day! Imagine a HAPPY, JOYFUL, CELEBRATORY Church service where people openly wept out of overwhelming joy every day!

I know several people who hold doctorate degrees from the most highly regarded seminaries who know absolutely nothing about the nature of Jesus, and even less about the scriptures.

SEMINARIANS

NOTE: I am fully aware that some readers will read this piece and judge my motive to be jealousy or competition, because I am not a graduate of a seminary and have never attended one. Nothing could be farther from the truth.

I believe that seminaries could be the most powerful institutions in the world if they were about one thing and one thing only: THE WORDS OF JESUS. Think of the great good that could be done if the focus of our spiritual education was on the Gospel of Jesus only.

I wrote this piece only as an example of how false teaching imbedded in traditions gets propagated and multiplied. Graduates of Seminaries are widely regarded as expert theologians by virtue of the degrees they hold. Some are, but many are absolutely not Bible scholars.

Once, a graduate Jesuit seminarian who after graduation decided not to accept ordination, came to my Bible study group. He was astonished at John 1:1–3. He told me that he had never been taught that elementary scripture.

"In the beginning was the Word and the Word was with God and the Word was God."

Seminarians learn many things like church management and semantics, similes, rhetoric, liturgy, homiletics, hermeneutics, exegesis, doctrines, church history, canon laws, philosophy, sacraments, etc. Don't misunderstand me. It's important to learn how to deliver a sermon.

There is certainly no harm in studying philosophy. It's not the curriculum that concerns me as much as the level of priority of Word Knowledge. Seminarians can learn more about the thought process of Socrates than that of Jesus. I honestly know one recent graduate of a denominational seminary who believes in abortion in every form including partial birth abortion, even up to the time of delivery.

Seminaries are the training grounds for church pastors. The students, like us, only know what they learn and have been taught. Since understanding and knowing how to correctly divide the Word is not their highest priority, graduates go forth and propagate the same ignorance that remains with them.

I know a great man who holds a doctorate from the most preeminent "Christian" seminary in America. The man actually believes that God burns houses down to teach that people do not need material things.

Still another graduate of the same institution teaches his flock that God intentionally steals things from them to teach them a lesson. He literally believes that the "Good" Lord gives and takes away. Seems like a conundrum to me.

Still another graduate of that institution believes that if you quote the power scriptures, you are attempting to manipulate God.

CHURCH PASTORS

Men who Pastor churches are, for the most part, salt of the earth folk. Their sacrifices are many. Their hearts are pure. Managing a church is one of the most difficult jobs there is. There are committee meetings, visitations, weddings, funerals, financial management, all kinds of internal politics and perpetual murmuring that must be handled.

The management of the building and premises and fund raising consume a large amount of time and effort. Managing a congregation is the definition of herding rabbits. It takes a very dedicated and special person to volunteer for this duty. I couldn't do it for one minute.

I admire and respect anyone willing to take on these responsibilities. That said, think how little time a church minister has to deeply study the Gospel or spend quality time with the Holy Spirit. In addition to all the chores listed above, the church minister must also pay attention to his family, manage familial responsibilities, and build in downtime to remain healthy mentally and physically.

The stress levels are overwhelming even for the leader of the smallest congregations. The minister of a smaller congregation may even have more stress, because the heaviest workloads go un-delegated. It's all up to him.

Stress is why so many wonderful preachers get divorced. Stress comes from low incomes and the pressures of running a church. It's hard to focus on the truth of the Gospel when your income is insufficient to meet your family's needs. Unfortunately, that is often the case.

Understanding the deepest meaning of the teachings of the Holy Spirit and Jesus's teachings requires constant, intentional, deliberate study.

Here again, Teacher Ron Reeser's favorite scripture:

BE CAREFUL what you are hearing. The measure of thought and study you give to the truth you hear will be the measure of virtue and knowledge that comes back to you—and more will be given to you who hear.

For to him who has will more (virtue and knowledge) be given; and from him who has nothing, even what he has will be taken away by force. (Mark 4–24)

These words are as true for preachers as they are for others. Actually even more so. You cannot give away what you don't have.

NO TIME TO LEARN THE WORD, TOO BUSY!

I went to a major league baseball game last night. There were 40,000 plus folk there having a great time. The process of going, finding seats, and returning took from 6:00 p.m. to about 11:00 p.m., about five hours. That happens every day.

Yet, I hear many people proclaim that to spend more than twenty minutes with the Lord, reading a teaching or watching a video, is just too much. People have warned me about the need to shorten this book. They have said that "people don't read books anymore."

WE MAKE TIME FOR WHAT IS IMPORTANT TO US.

The evil liar is all about keeping us ignorant of the Word. One way he does this is by distracting us with the urgent. There is a book titled *The Tyranny Of The Urgent* by Charles E. Hummel. That title says it all. When we are blown to and fro by circumstances and what we perceive to be the immediate need to deal with them, we have little time for God or His Word.

The vast majority of folk learn the Word from the pulpit. They prefer to let the preacher do their research and study for them. That is not how one builds a deep personal relationship with Jesus.

Too many of Jesus's sheep are led by the words of the preacher, instead of investigating, learning, and being led by the knowledge of the Word of God.

THE CURE FOR IGNORANCE IS STUDY!

UNBELIEF

Unbelief is mostly a choice or decision. If is often a thought planted in minds by you know who that modern people are so sophisticated they are actually smarter than the God of the Bible. Those who choose not to believe sometimes make that decision, because they enjoy their Godless amoral lives and choose not to change.

Some people are like alcoholics who just do not want to stop drinking and resent anything or anyone who gets in the way. Some people choose not to believe because of the garbage they have heard from the pulpit. Some unbelievers want nothing to do with a God who would kill a child or burn down a house to teach people or would allow cancer or Alzheimer's to exist; and they have been taught that He does by those who purport to represent Him. Some unbelievers want nothing to do with a God who would take a good job away from a person to teach them something or kill their mother or hate certain groups of people. Neither would I.

Could you bring yourself to believe a God who sent a hurricane to punish the sinners in one part of a city, and wiped out the homes of thousands of people in three states?

Many unbelievers want nothing to do with the mean-ass, cruel, brutal, merciless, punishing, judging, and condemning god that they have heard about through the church or it's disciples.

A church man told me one time that his plan was to beat the hell out of his children because God beats the hell out of His. Nobody wants any part of that!

MINISTERS, TEACHERS, EVANGELISTS, MISSIONARIES

Many ministers/evangelists/teachers/missionaries just do not believe the Gospel. They believe parts of the Gospel. They believe the scriptures that support their world view and religious paradigms and traditions.

The unedited Gospel of Jesus is beyond their capacity to believe, understand, and teach. If this were not true, we would see their fruit. Preachers do not teach what they do not believe, so ignorance is perpetuated on their flocks and those they come in contact with. Ignorance multiplies exponentially. Unbelief causes ignorance to live and prosper.

Some church leaders can't bring themselves to accept the promises of Jesus for a host of reasons, not the least of which is the cost to them personally and professionally

GREED—FOLLOW THE MONEY

There are some people in the pulpit who are just evil. They are not interested in empowering God's flock. They are interested in gaining wealth, status, power, and acclamation from a heart of pure greed or unabated narcissism.

Please understand this: I believe that Apostles, Prophets, Evangelists, Pastors, and Teachers should be well compensated. There is no reason why a Lawyer or Doctor or Finance Manager should be paid more than a man of the cloth. I do not even have a problem with Pastors being rewarded by their flock in millions of dollars if their purpose is to bless God. I do have a problem with men who teach works to gain wealth. I do have a problem with clergy whose motive is cleaning out the widow.

This is not about your Pastor. It is about charlatans, scammers, blowhards, and teachers who have no conscience. It is about those who are grossly overpaid for perpetuating a bastardized version of the Gospel.

My uncle Jim, who is a WWII hero and looks like a handsomer version of John Wayne, still has his service .45. He was once appointed usher at his Baptist church.

When it came time for the collection, as the offering plates were being passed along, he opened his jacket. Then he pointed to his gun which hung from his shoulder holster. Of course, the gun was not loaded. Every time I think about that incident, I crack up. Of course he was just out for a laugh, but there is much truth in that episode.

EXTORTION is an important tool for some ministries. It is the instrument of choice for the people that I resent. God does not want offerings which are given grudgingly or out of necessity or followers who come to Him in fear of not accepting him or in fear of punishment.

He does not want folk to come to Him grudgingly or out of necessity or as a result of bullying or arm twisting.

A teaching on giving from the Holy Spirit through Paul:

Remember this: he who sows sparingly and grudgingly will also reap sparingly and grudgingly, and he who sows generously will also reap generously and with blessing. Let each one give as he has made up his own mind and proposed in his heart, NOT RELUCTANTLY OR SORROWFULLY OR UNDER COMPULSION, for God takes pleasure in prizes above other things, and is unwilling to abandon or to do without a CHEERFUL,

JOYOUS prompt to do it giver whose heart is in his giving.
(2 Corinthians 9:7)

HERE COMES THE GREED PART

I am not going to name names, but look up the highest paid pastors in the world.

You will see net worth's ranging from $500,000 to $26,000,000. I know what most of them teach and who they are. I have heard their dogma.

For many, their modus operandi is separating gullible but honest people seeking a good relationship with Jesus, from their money. They impose on their flock a scripture that never had anything to do with anybody but Levitical Priests (Malachi 3:9–10).

There was a Prophet who loved God with all of his heart. He was the last Prophet to the nation of Israel. His name was Malachi. Malachi asked God how Israel could get back in God's favor and good graces.

Malachi was a Levitical Priest. The Levitical Priests were charged with collecting a tithe, ten percent of the wealth of Israel. They were supposed to use the money to purchase food and store it in barns. The Levites were one of the twelve tribes of Israel. They were sons of Levi.

Instead, they stole the money and goods, and used it for their own personal enrichment. What the Priests did was paw the honey jar and use the money for their own desires. The result was that there was not enough food for the people.

Here is God's response to Malachi:

Even from the days of your fathers you have turned aside from My ordinances and have not kept them. Return to me, and I will return to you, says the Lord of Hosts. But you say, "How shall we return?" Will a man rob or defraud God? Yet, you rob and defraud Me. But you say, "In what way do we rob and defraud You?" You have withheld your tithes and offerings.

You are cursed with the curse, for you are robbing Me, even this whole nation. "Bring all the tithes (the whole tenth of your income) into the storehouse that there may be food in MY house. Test me in this and see if I will not open the windows of heaven for you and pour you out a blessing that there shall not be room enough to receive it.

And I will rebuke the devourer (old scratch) for your sakes, and he shall not destroy the fruits of your ground (using insects and plaques), neither shall your vine drop its fruit before the time in the field. (Malachi 3:7–11)

Today, the wolves and haranguers use this scripture to extort millions of dollars from their hornswoggled congregants and viewers. They shout through their swollen Nostrils, to their marks, "If you don't give ten percent of your gross income, YOU WILL BE ROBBING GOD! AND YOU WILL BECOME ACCURSED!"

The scared, fretful, quivering succors throw open their wallets and purses and retirement money, and pour hundreds of millions on these vermin. The victims certainly are not to blame. Their intention is to bless God with their first fruits.

What the flocks get in return for their purloined shekels is a watered down half-truth filled monologue that fractures and minimizes the promises of Jesus.

That message from God was intended only for and delivered only to the Levitical priests and the sons of Arron who were short sheeting God. It has now been weaponized by shysters.

Malachi 3 has nothing whatsoever to do with giving!

IT IS ABOUT THOSE WHO STEAL THE OFFERINGS OF THE GIVERS.

One diluted perp who runs one of the biggest Baptist arenas in America stood up in the pulpit and went full bore on this crap.

He shouted at his bewildered sheep, "If even one of you is not giving this church at least ten percent of your gross income, get up, walk out, and never return, because you thieves are robbing God."

You would think the frozen, weak kneed flock would all get up and walk out en masse—wrong!

A friend who attended that service told me that his congregation sat shivering in their pews and began fervently doling out the dough to old Reverend Capone.

Now with his ill-gotten gains, his church is bigger, and I mean bigger and more grand than ever. It seems the harder this dude cracks the whip on his submissive flock, the more they like it. He manages a flock of nearly 20,000.

TELEVANGELISTS

Another Disclaimer: Not All Evangelists Are Crooked. Some are very noble.

The Gospel of Jesus is totally irrelevant to crooked evangelists. They started their racket back in the circus days. That is where they honed their craft. They started renting tents in small towns and raking the hopeful seeking "Revival."

Then there was radio and "Put your hands on the radio and shout it if you believe it!"

Then along came the cathode ray tube. It was the perfect venue. Television worked like a charm. Just buy some time on local stations who needed the money and blubber away.

I can still see in my mind's eye these dramatic actors. No thespian could hold a candle to them. They were prolific criers. Their flummery got slicker and slicker. Weeping seemed to be an art of the craft. Some of these flamboyant flimflammers became highly skilled boo-hoo pros. These bamboozlers had at least ten "Healing Miracles" at every broadcast.

One of them elevated gut-wrenching sobbing to an art form of the caliber of Michael Angelo. Night after night comes the rain. He must rub onions in his eyes before every service, but my how the money rolls in. This dude is very old and very rich.

Fast forward to the Cable Networks. Cable television was invented, and there was nothing stopping them from sapping millions of joyous onlookers in a mere half hour.

With cable television, the belly crawlers went from screwing the flock out of two or three million a year to twenty or thirty million a year.

Jimmy the Zyppah and Sham Wow guy looks like a rank amateur in comparison to these Hoo Do's.

One of these cats in the Midwest must be coked up when he attacks the airwaves. Hellfire and brimstone billows as he bellows! I believe I may have seen him blow flames and smoke out of his ears. Several times, I thought that he might suffer a massive physical explosion during one of his astonishing rants. I don't see how his huge audience can stand it. I would be terrorized that the dude might literally explode.

KING JESUS SPOKE OF THEM LIKE THIS

A good tree cannot bear bad fruit nor can a bad tree bear excellent fruit. Every tree that does not bear good fruit is cut down and cast into the fire. Therefore, you will fully know them by their fruits.

Not all who say to Me, "Lord, Lord," will enter the Kingdom of heaven. But he who does the will of My Father Who is in heaven. Many will say to me in that day, "Lord, Lord, have we not prophesied in Your name and driven out demons in Your name and done many mighty works in your name?"

And then I will say to them openly, publicly, "I never knew you: depart from me, you who act wickedly." (Matthew 7:18–23)

That warning was intended for these bellicose twerps, who spit in Jesus's face every day. They are the whitewashed tombs and broods of vipers about whom you have read that Jesus ate alive.

One of the wealthiest, if not the wealthiest, slobbering con artists is a dude that has revival meetings that are a three ring circus. He coils up like the snake he is and calls to his precipitous stage, all who are "ailing." He saunters up to them and smacks them on the head, and shouts, "You are healed!" From the power of the swat on the noggin from this "Highly Anointed" hobnob, the recipient of the miraculous recovery "is slain in the Spirit," in the parlance of the slimy frauds.

Many folks are actually slain in the Spirit at some very legitimate honest ministries. That is not who I am writing about.

Momentarily, the participants throw away their wheelchairs and walkers, and skip around the stage rejoicing at the power of the Big Cheese. The silly man is known around the world. If this scurrilous knave knew anything about the Gospel of Jesus, He would know that his yammering and shouting and slapping means absolutely nothing.

IT IS IMPOSSIBLE TO HEAL A PERSON!

Yes, Jesus did say that a sign of those who believe in Him is that they will lay hands on the sick and the sick shall recover. He was speaking to those who had not yet received His power and promises, because He had not yet finished His work.

You can buck and kick and squirm and dance, but your nonsense has no effect. You can lather them up with anointing oil, you can pray until you are purple, you can shout to the rooftop, you can dance and roll in the floor, you can lay "anointed" hands on people, you can spit in their eye; but you can never heal them!

You can make them hear and hear until they go deaf. Until a person makes a decision to believe that they were healed by Jesus on the cross, and believe without doubt that He died from every disease known and unknown to man by taking all of them into His body, nothing will happen.

He Personally bore our sins in His own body on the cross as on an altar and offered Himself on it, that we might die to sin and live to righteousness. BY HIS WOUNDS YOU HAVE BEEN HEALED. (1 Peter 2:24)

SURELY HE HAS borne our griefs (maladies, infirmities, diseases, sicknesses, and distresses), and carried our sorrows and pains of punishment. yet we ignorantly considered Him stricken, smitten and afflicted by God. But He was wounded for our transgressions, He was bruised for our guilt and iniquities the punishment needful to obtain peace and well-being for us was upon Him, and with the stripes that wounded Him we are healed and made whole. (Isaiah 53:4–5)

The healing came in the first part when He bore all diseases known and unknown to man in His body on the cross, thereby destroying them and their power once and forever.

His stripes were the punishment for our sins, and by them we were forgiven of all of our sins past, present, and future, ONCE AND FOR ALL!

Therefore, asking God to heal a person or trying to heal a person or asking for forgiveness is the ultimate insult to Jesus and God, and is a profound statement of unbelief.

Can anointing oil do something that Jesus has already done? Can you pray in tongues and heal an already healed person? Can you slap a person into being healed when Jesus healed them 2000 years ago?

You certainly can receive the healing that Jesus gave you on the cross by faith! But using your faith to heal a person is spiritual nonsense.

YES, HEALING COMES THROUGH FAITH! It comes through the free gift of faith given you by Jesus. But it does not come through any man or woman or their acts or behaviors.

One minister/teacher/televangelist that is very honest and well-intended has a healing school, and believes that people are healed by the laying on of hands. This is a major point on which we part company theologically.

People tell me that when they listen to this man, he sounds "just like" me. Not hardly; it's hard to get me to believe your grace message if you bring healing under works.

BACK TO THE CARNIVAL

These manipulators and conmen are not of Jesus. How can you claim to serve Jesus and that He is the King of your life, and make a living duping His flock?

Worse, they give Jesus a black eye! The image they paint of the King of Kings is loathsome and another excuse for people to avoid or refuse to believe Him.

What could St. Jude's or the Aflac children's cancer center or the Shrine's burns hospital or the Ronald McDonald house do with the billions that get sent to these profiteers? Frequently, these men pray on their television shows for the poor. One who is worth close to a billion dollars, the richest of all, does it regularly.

It is no different than fabulously rich liberals who live in guarded, fenced, gated mansions, decrying the lack of interest in the homeless and gun control and greenhouse emissions.

Have you seen even one of them move into a tent and live without air conditioning or sell their cars and give the money to the poor? Can you imagine one of the elitist Hollywood folk living without armed security or an entourage to protect them? If either group were actually so stridently concerned about the poor and huddled masses, why wouldn't they give all their money to the Salvation Army or just dole it out to the homeless on the street?

THE HOLY SPIRIT WARNED US

Heed these Prophetic Words directed by the Holy Spirit and written by Paul to his protégé, Timothy. Paul was in prison in chains in Rome as he wrote this highly accurate prophecy:

BUT UNDERSTAND this that the last days will come set in perilous times of great stress and trouble, hard to deal with and hard to bear.

For people will be lovers of self and utterly self-centered lovers of money and aroused by and inordinate greedy desire for wealth, proud and arrogant and contemptuous boasters.

They will be abusive, blasphemous, scoffing, disobedient to parents, ungrateful, unholy and profane.

They will be without natural human affection, callous and inhuman, relentless admitting of no truce or appeasement they will be slanderers, false accusers, trouble makers, intemperate and loose in morals and conduct, uncontrolled and fierce, haters of good.

They will be treacherous betrayers, rash, inflated with self-conceit. They will be lovers of sensual pleasures and vain amusements more than and rather than lovers of God.

Here comes the description of bogus church leaders of today who are in it to win it.

For though they hold a piety true religion, they deny and reject and are strangers to the power of it. Their conduct belies the genuineness of their profession. Avoid all such people, turn away from them.

Sadly, far too many preachers today teach works and performance, and at the same time deny the power promises of Jesus.

For among them are those who worm their way into homes and captivate silly and weak natured and spiritually dwarfed women, loaded down with the burden of their sins and easily swayed and led away by evil desires and seductive impulses.

These weak women will listen to anybody who will teach them; they are forever inquiring and getting information, but are never able to arrive at a recognition and knowledge of the Truth. (2 Timothy 3:1–7)

This is not condemnation of any woman. It is an accurate portrayal of the evil perpetuated on many women by scurrilous, motivated evil slime. It is not about all women. It is about "weak" women.

The Holy Spirit is not attacking women. He is shining the light of truth on these disgusting worms who mislead them and con them. Women are clearly not at fault. Their deceivers, though, are bound for hell.

JESUS BLASTING HYPOCRITES

The scribes and the Pharisees sit on Moses' seat (Seats of Honor), *so practice and observe whatever they tell you* (The Jews were under the authority of the Priests, because they rejected God for a king and laws, so they were required to obey them) *but not what they do. For they preach, but do not practice.*

They tie up heavy burdens (rules and regulations much as do the leaders of today) *and lay them on people's shoulders, but they themselves are not willing to move them with their finger.*

They do all their deeds to be seen by others, for they make their phylacteries broad and their fringes long, and they love the place of honor at feasts and the best seats in the synagogues and greetings in the marketplaces and to be called Rabbi by others.

By way of explanation, Phylacteries are leather pouches containing key scriptures from the first five books of the Torah. We call those books the Pentateuch. They were attached to the left arm, forehead, and the heart by straps. Virtually every Jewish man over the age of thirteen wore them during prayer time. They are still worn today.

The Egotistical Pharisees and Scribes and Sadducees expanded the width of the straps to show off. They wore them not just at prayer time, but wherever they went, to be seen and admired by the flock. And to be admired and honored for their devoutness. They were tooting their own horns and implying that they were far more pious than anyone else.

All teachers and Rabbis wore robes with sky blue fringe around the hem of the garment as a symbol of their faith in God. The fat-headed leaders expanded their fringe as a display of ostentatiousness.

Both of these acts were designed to project themselves as being much more devout than others. They were about seeking admiration and the highest esteem.

Today, people build huge monolithic churches for the same reason. Their church has to be the biggest and baddest. Their church has to have the biggest organ in town.

SONS OF HELL

BUT WOE TO YOU, scribes and Pharisees, pretenders for you travel over sea and land to make a single convert, and when he becomes one you make him *DOUBLY AS MUCH A CHILD OF HELL AS YOU ARE.*

These are the preachers of today who are no different. They devote much of their work to finding new converts and new members for their spiritual labor camps.

When they get them, they place them under a performance-based relationship with God. The burdens they place on these folk are unbearable, and they are impossible to fulfill. That is why so many leave or never attend church, and despise "Organized Religion."

The blind guides of today teach their flock crap like "God is in control, God giveth and God taketh away, God only helps those who help themselves," and all of the Holy Cows you read about in our first chapter.

Jesus called these people, "CHILDREN OF HELL." And people think that I am too blunt and accusatory.

SOME EXAMPLES

There is one old dusty butt tele-preacher who owns a brand new multimillion-dollar Citation 10 Jet, which he uses to travel the world over, binding Gentiles and Christians to the law of Moses that never has applied to them and never will.

The deep pockets keep blowing big bucks into his "ministry," because He is a very rich and "successful" man. His church is magnificent and beautiful, and it smells good.

There is one international evangelist who goes to Africa and leases huge tracts of land. He uses areas several football fields in size. He places massive loud speakers on telephone poles and has the tribal leaders, through whatever means necessary, drag their villagers and all of the people of the neighboring villages to his rallies.

When the confused natives show up, he shouts hellfire and damnation at them in broken English through a translator and the huge speakers. The poor victims huddle in fear of hellfire and damnation. The rant and verbal harangue goes on for hours. The coerced attendees are in shock and awe of this loudmouth.

He literally scares the hell out of them. They don't want to burn in hell. As they leave, his workers shove a signature card at them and make them sign if they can write; if not, any mark will do—a statement that they have accepted Jesus.

After the rally, the "millions" of signed acceptance cards are collected and used to prove to big donors that this man is leading "millions" of Godless natives of the "Dark Continent" to Jesus. Few Americans have seen this snake wail. If you ever had seen his bellicose rant, you would think that he was a demonic psychopath. He sells fear and he is good at it.

RELIGION SELLS FEAR! JESUS BRINGS PEACE!

As soon as the big Kahuna packs up his speakers and leaves, it's all over. The native villagers have no clue what they just did or what comes next. They just signed up with Jesus, they were pressured into throwing their little money into a giant bucket, but they have no idea what that means or what to do next. All they know is that their pockets are more empty than before they went to the rally. Great program! Never Fails! Millions roll in!

THE CARES OF THIS WORLD

The fear of what others will think of me!

Certainly one of the reasons you have never heard the true Gospel of Jesus as you read in this book is that Pastors, Church Leaders, Elders, Deacons, and Sunday School Teachers want to build big flocks.

Teaching the Gospel of Jesus is controversial. Jesus's true Gospel is not popular, and to build that 20,000-member flock, we must be non-controversial and popular.

The desire to be well thought of is BIG BUSINESS. Big time business people donate to big churches to be seen as being involved with a successful operation. They presume that the more grandiose the building and television network, the more excellent the organization must be. They want their man to be young and physically fit. The more Kennedy-like the teeth, the more financially attractive. Their boy must be super cool, suave, and sophisticated. Because that is how they see themselves. Appearance isn't just the thing; it's the only thing.

MONEY ATTRACTS MONEY! If you are part of the deep pocket First Church of Commerce, there are great opportunities to align with and sell your goods and services to other "Daddy War Bucks."

Many regular Jane's and Joe's prefer mega and popular churches, because they think the Pastor must be blessed and of high standing with God. How else, they think, could his church have grown so large?

Parents seek large successful churches for their children's sakes. They need to be with like-minded families and their kids. I am frequently told by parents who knowingly attend churches whose theology is antithetical to the Gospel of Jesus and don't care about the message. They want their children to be where there are lots of other kids their age.

The more books, CD's, videotapes and such that the leader of these "Churches" write and sell, the more attractive the organization becomes to high net worth donors.

"Winners" want to be a part of a winning team. They attend popular brand name churches to be seen and to meet other big business folk. It's sort of an incestuous networking cycle, and it works. The grander the outward appearance, the greater the offerings from the well-off. The result is that the big brand name churches who feed their flocks pabulum and/or works grow and grow. The inaccuracy of content is irrelevant. Coolness is the key!

And the veil of ignorance is hung before the clouded eyes of millions of Jesus's people in perpetuity. Correct teaching of the Gospel matters not. Coolness is the thing.

A BROOD OF VIPERS

Political and socially correct churches, those who will not teach the power scriptures of the Gospel of Jesus, the money grubbing con artists who fleece the flock of Jesus, those who know the truth and will not teach it—all of these are no different than the Pharisees, Sadducees, and the Scribes surrounding Jesus while He was here.

Jesus called them all a "BROOD OF VIPERS." By the by, whenever Jesus talks about vipers, He is referring to satan or his henchmen or his demons or his angels.

But woe to you scribes and Pharisees, hypocrites! For you shut the kingdom of heaven in people's faces (by making the requirements to gain entrance to heaven, impossible to achieve).

But woe to you, scribes and Pharisees, pretenders, hypocrites! For you shut the kingdom of heaven in men's faces; for you neither enter yourselves, nor do you allow those who are about to go in to do so.

Woe to you, scribes and Pharisees, pretenders! For you swallow up widows' houses and for a pretense to cover it up make long prayers; therefore, you will receive the greater condemnation and the heavier sentence.

The multimillionaire wolves in sheep's clothing, who extort and rob and blow hellfire on Jesus's peeps, are about to reap what they have sown.

Read Jesus shouting at the charlatans of His day and ours:

"You Serpents, You spawn of vipers! How can you escape the penalty to be suffered in Hell?"

PAY ATTENTION! Jesus is stating clearly that those who teach a Gospel that is not His are in the employ and service of their father, satan.

"Woe to you, scribes and Pharisees, hypocrites! For you are like whitewashed tombs, which outwardly appear to be beautiful, but within are full of dead people's bones and all uncleanness. So you outwardly appear righteous to others, but within you are full of hypocrisy and lawlessness."

Sadly, there are far too many bones of dead people under the whitewashed tombs of the spiritual leaders of today! They have the blood of the ignorant on their hands!

The scriptures I just quoted are slightly out of context, but all come from the twenty-third chapter of Matthew. Read it! It is so cool! It is the original "come to Jesus" meeting.

ALL GOOD THINGS COME TO AN END

NOW YOUR LIFE WILL NEVER BE THE SAME. You are no longer ignorant of your inheritance. You now know that you have the same power as Jesus, and the responsibility to use it.

Now you know that you have ALREADY BEEN GIVEN ALL THINGS THAT PERTAIN TO LIFE AND GODLINESS. Now you know that satan is nothing but a malignant growth. You know that you have been given authority over him and all of his servants. You know now that the burnt-up devil is nothing but a damned liar. You know now that he has no power.

Now you know that Jesus hears and speaks to you constantly. You know that Jesus will never leave you or forsake you, and that you can now come BOLDLY BEFORE THE THRONE OF GRACE to obtain mercy and find grace to help in a time of need.

Now you know that Jesus replaced the 613 Hebrew laws and ordinances that only applied to the Jews, and only until Jesus came with His Salvation and Grace. Now you know that we gentiles have been saved by grace through faith.

Now you know that you have Jesus's faith and you cannot grow it, expand it, multiply it, stretch it, hear and hear and get more of it.

Now you know that because you have the faith of Jesus, your faith is entire, lacking nothing. Now you know that our precious King loves you eternally and will never leave you or forsake you. Now you know that Jesus Ain't Gonna Do Nothin and why. Now you know that you have been healed, forgiven, been made a joint heir with Jesus, become a son or daughter of God. Now you know that you have been forgiven—past, present, and future.

Now you know that GOD IS LOVE. Now you know that God is not keeping a record of your sins. Now you know that God is not judging or condemning you. Now you know that God loves everything that He has created. Now you know that nothing can separate us from the LOVE OF GOD.

Now, friends, you know who, what, why, and how the truth has been denied you to this point. Now you know the truth, the whole truth, and nothing but the truth. Our hope is that you will receive and employ all of the blessings and powers that you have inherited, to change your life and those of all you come in contact with!

Jesus and I agree that you will now choose a happy, joyful, healthy, prosperous, good life filled with the LOVE of your King.

Jesus and I pray that you will invite all who are dear to you to join you in eternal joy and peace by accepting Jesus and His "GOOD NEWS OF GREAT JOY THAT SHALL BE TO ALL THE PEOPLE!"

The Holy Spirit and I are in agreement that you now know that God, The Holy Spirit, and Jesus are nothing like you thought they were when you began this teaching. Surely, you have learned the true nature of our precious King. Surely you have seen a glimmer of how much you are loved by Him.

Jesus and I agree that you have chosen not to gamble on you being smarter than God. Jesus and I agree that you have thoroughly weighed the pros and cons of accepting Jesus in your life, and having done so, realize that you have absolutely nothing to lose and everything to gain by simply accepting Jesus as your king.

If you have just done so, remember that all you need do to accept Jesus is to tell Him that you believe in Him, and that He is your king. If you just did that, you are as saved as Billy Graham. Congratulations. Your life is about to change in glorious ways that you never dreamed possible. Surely, goodness and mercy will follow you all the days of your life, and you will dwell in the house of the Lord forever and ever.

Never Forget Jesus's Words:

"IT IS *FINISHED"*

That is why JESUS AIN'T GONNA DO NOTHIN'!

12

Thank You

On behalf of the Father, The Son and The Holy Spirit, and The Word, Thank You!

Thank you for not quitting! You are a champion!

Thank you for not receiving a spirit of offense as you took hold of the truth.

Thank you for becoming willing to at least consider the True Gospel of Jesus.

Special thanks to you if you were atheist, agnostic or nihilist or of another faith, but held your nose and pressed on. Each of you are so important to Jesus and to me. We want to see you make a decision to live forever and not perish. Please remember, you have nothing at all to lose by accepting Jesus. For those of different religions or philosophies, does the religion you follow guarantee, without any doubt, your eternal salvation? Is it possible for you to meet the requirement of your religion completely?

Please ask yourself if you have ever sinned in thought or in deed. Then ask yourself the price of that sin without an atoning sacrifice. The Holy Spirit spoke to the children of Israel and told them that without the shedding of blood, there is no atonement.

If you do not atone for your sins through the only sinless person who ever lived, how will you pay the total price and consequences of those sins?

Please ask yourself if any man has ever claimed to be God, other than Jesus. Ask yourself if any person, other than Jesus, has died to pay for your sins. Ask yourself if the God of any other religion has ever demonstrated a purer love than to live the indignity of a human life, walk through life being tempted with everything we are, yet did not sin. Ask yourself if any other God could possibly relate to the pain and suffering and temptation that you have been exposed to.

Finally, ask yourself if any other God loved His followers enough to walk the earth for thirty-three years as a human, then died the most horrid death possible to heal and forgive His children as a demonstration of the unqualified love He has for them—Buddha, Confucius, Allah, The sun God or the evil one?

Thank you for learning that God is not mean or hateful; rather, He is the essence of LOVE.

Thank you for accepting Jesus's unending love for you!

Thank you for accepting Jesus and making Him your King of Kings and Lord of Lords. Thank you for inviting Him to live in your heart.

Thank you for accepting eternal salvation and eternal life with GOD, JESUS, THE HOLY SPIRIT AND THEIR WORD in Their World, Heaven.

Thank you for repenting, letting go, and changing your old beliefs in exchange for the truth. Thank you for letting go of your work-based life. Thank you for letting go of traditions and dogma and religion.

Thank you for accepting the power of Jesus and determining to use it!

Thank you for receiving newness of life.

Thank you for accepting the free gift of the Peace, Mercy, and Grace of Jesus.

Thank you for believing that the evil one is powerless except to lie in the lives of the followers of Jesus.

Thank you for receiving and employing dominion over the devil and ALL of those who serve him.

Thank you for receiving, by faith, the free gift of "All Things That Pertain To Life and Godliness."

Thank you for accepting the forgiveness that Jesus paid for with His blood.

Thank you for accepting the healing that Jesus died a horrible, ghastly death to give you.

Thank you for receiving the free gift of the fullness of the faith of Jesus.

Thank you for committing, with all of your being, to never again ask God for the things that He gave you and that have been paid in full and purchased for you with His Blood.

Thank you for helping the Holy Spirit spread this Love letter to as many people as possible all over the earth.

Thank you for fact-checking this love letter by searching the scriptures.

Thank you for falling in Love with our King.

Thank you for becoming willing to accept the truth and to change. That means to forgo old non-biblical paradigms. Thank you for joining me in killing old holy cows and non-biblical clichés.

Thank you for putting away your old self and putting on your newly regenerated self. It is never too late to change.

Thank you for living eternally with Jesus while beaming His love to as many as you can! I cannot wait to meet and speak with each of you in heaven. What a great party we will have!

Thank You! You are God's glorious inheritance! You are what He inherits. He gave you everything; give Him you.

May you live forever in the Loving arms of the One who created you!

PLEASE! IF YOU LIKE THIS BOOK AND AGREE WITH THE MESSAGE, AND YOU WANT TO SEE IT READ BY AS MANY AS POSSIBLE, HELP US.

You can find our teachings in video, audio, and written formats at our fantastic website, KNOWJESUSKNOWGRACE.COM

We also have a Facebook page under that name. Please visit us, and if you are blessed by it, please like the page. Our teaching videos are posted on our Facebook page and on YouTube under Pastor ALLEN FLEMING.

Throne of Grace Ministries is a 501(c)(3) independent ministry. We are not funded by any outside group or denomination. We are entirely funded by the generosity of our loving, generous givers.

Every gift is deeply needed and appreciated, no matter how small or great. A five-dollar offering is as appreciated as a million dollar plus one.

We would be so blessed to have you join our team! You can help us by sending your tax exempt offering to:

Throne of Grace

P.O.BOX 669153

Marietta, Georgia 30066

THANK YOU!

Pastor Allen Fleming, on behalf of The Holy Spirit!

About the Author

In the beginning was the Word (Jesus), and the Word was with God, and the Word was God Himself.

Jesus said, "I am the Way and the Truth and the Life, no one comes to the Father but by Me. If you had known Me (had learned to recognize Me), you would also have known My Father. From now on, you know Him and have seen Him."

The Holy Spirit indwells us when we make a decision to honestly make Jesus the ruler of our lives, the director of our play. The Holy Spirit is as much God as the Word, Jesus, and God the Father. They—The Word, The Father, The Holy Spirit, and Jesus are all one and the same in different, yet equal parts.

God in the person of the Holy Spirit asked me to write this book. God in the person of Jesus made the scriptures. The Holy Spirit dictated the scriptures and content to me. God in all four persons created this book. I am merely the typist.

Pastor Allen Fleming made a serious decision to make Jesus his King on February 27, 1987. Jesus helped Him gain sobriety from the wonderful program of Alcoholics Anonymous on August 26, 1986. Pastor Allen has been intensely studying the Word under the Direction of his instructor, The Holy Spirit, since the day he surrendered his life to Jesus.

Allen began his ministry counseling, sponsoring, guiding, and teaching the Good News of the Gospel of Jesus to fellow alcoholics in 1988. In 1999, he was ordained and in 2002, started KNOWJESUSKNOWGRACE.COM Throne of Grace Ministries, Inc. with his partner Mike C.

His first book, What If Jesus Told the Truth, is available on Amazon. On the website, there are more than 200 written, video, and audio teachings. TOG ministers to 95,000 people in more than 100 countries around the World via the internet every year.